Throwing the Emperor from His Horse

Portrait of a Village Leader in China, 1923–1995

Peter J. Seybolt

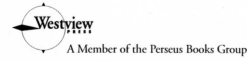
Westview
PRESS

A Member of the Perseus Books Group

Published in 1996 in the United States of America by Westview Press, 5500 Central Avenue, Boulder, Colorado 80301-2877, and in the United Kingdom by Westview Press, 12 Hid's Copse Road, Cumnor Hill, Oxford OX2 9JJ

Library of Congress Cataloging-in-Publication Data
Seybolt, Peter
    Throwing the emperor from his horse : portrait of a village leader
in China, 1923–1995 / Peter J. Seybolt.
        p.   cm.
    Includes bibliographical references.
    ISBN 0-8133-3130-7 (hc) —ISBN 0-8133-3131-5 (pb)
    1. Wang, Fucheng, 1923–1925.   2. Houhua Village (China)—
Biography.   3. Houhua Village (China)—History.   I. Title.
CT1828.W318S49   1996
951′.18—dc20
[B]   96-32797
                                                                                     CIP

Text design by Heather Hutchison

For Cynthia

翁下一身剐

敢把皇帝拉下写

"At the risk of death, dare to throw the emperor from his horse."

The title of this book is taken from a traditional Chinese aphorism based on the Confucian principle that a person of integrity, that is, one who acts in accordance with universal moral imperatives, will have the courage to risk his life challenging those in positions of authority who are misusing their power. Mao Zedong, Chairman of the Communist Party of China, quoted the aphorism during the Cultural Revolution in the 1960s when exhorting people to overthrow the president of the country, Liu Shaoqi, and other leaders in the Party and government whose policies, he said, were counterrevolutionary. Wang Fucheng, the principal subject of this book, knew little of the political disputes that divided the top leadership of the Communist Party, but he admired the aphorism for its emphasis on integrity and courage—two personal characteristics that he sought to emulate as leader of his village. It was one of only two quotations from the sayings of Chairman Mao that Wang could remember when I interviewed him in the early 1990s.

Contents

Illustrations

Maps

Photos

Preface

Wang Fucheng,* the subject of this book, was born in 1923. For most of his life he lived in Houhua Village in northern Henan Province. His name does not appear in Chinese biographical dictionaries. It is not even included in accounts of prominent people in the local county gazetteer. Only in his village and the immediately surrounding area was he known. Within that small world he was respected but not famous. For thirty years, 1954–1984, he was Communist Party branch secretary, the highest office in his village. He served with competence, even distinction, though the scope of his activities and range of knowledge were limited by his total illiteracy.

Wang Fucheng knew little of the world beyond his village. Until the Communist Party introduced a campaign to criticize Confucius in 1971, Wang had never heard of the sage or his teaching. Even afterward, he still knew Confucius only by the deprecating title "Kong lao er" [Kong's second child] and was ignorant of when he lived or what he did. The best Wang Fucheng could offer when asked about Confucius was the remark, "I heard he was a big capitalist and landlord from Shandong Province who didn't participate in manual labor." Despite his official position in the Communist Party, Wang Fucheng was ignorant even of the names of many top Party leaders. Before I arrived in Houhua Village, Wang Fucheng had never seen a foreigner and had no idea of foreign ways. When I talked with officials of Liucun Township, the administrative level above Houhua Village, they wondered why I had chosen to write about Wang Fucheng. They made it clear that in their opinion there was nothing very special about him, and they conceded only that "he is a good example of local leadership from among the people."

One might well ask, "Why write a book about Wang Fucheng and Houhua Village? What is significant about this man and this place?" The answer requires some explanation.

In 1987 I went to northern Henan Province to study the effects of the "War of Resistance" (1937–1945)[1] there, especially as they influenced the rise of the Communist Party. I had done research on this topic in other

---

*Throughout this book, personal names of Chinese are rendered in the Chinese fashion, with the family name first.

parts of China for a number of years. Northern Henan was particularly interesting to me because of the complex situation there during the war. It had been the scene of continual struggle between various contending forces including the Communists, the Japanese, the Nationalist (Guomindang) government of China, and an assortment of local bandit gangs and secret religious societies. At various times, and in varying circumstances, individuals within all of these distinct entities collaborated with, as well as fought with, each other to gain political and economic advantage. Until the end of the war, no one contender had been able to establish firm control. The problems in northern Henan differed significantly from those in other areas where the rise of the Communist Party had been analyzed, but no one in the West had studied them,[2] principally because the area was economically backward and therefore closed to foreigners by the Chinese government. The opportunity to go there, arranged by a colleague after two years of negotiation with Chinese officials,[3] was too good to miss.

With the generous assistance of faculty in the History Department at Zhengzhou University (in Zhengzhou City, capital of Henan Province) I began collecting and reading materials on the history of northern Henan. I then took up residence in Puyang, a new city that has become the administrative center of the recently developed oil-drilling industry on the central plain of north China. From Puyang, I planned to travel to nearby villages of the "sand region" to interview peasants who remembered the war years. The sand region is distinguished by alluvial deposits from the Yellow River that formed when the river flowed through the area a millennium earlier. The quality of the fine, gritty soil is poor, but the wind-blown dunes and the Chinese date trees that grow on them provided rare cover on the otherwise flat plain for guerrilla activities during the war. The Communists had been especially active and successful there, and thus the area was of particular interest for my study.

Arranging village interviews in the sand region was no easy task. One first had to obtain permission from successive levels of the bureaucratic hierarchy, from province to county to township to village. Below the provincial level, all contact was in person, partly because that is the Chinese way and partly because mail service was slow and unreliable and telephones rarely worked. Making arrangements at county and township levels usually included an elaborate luncheon banquet at which there was much drinking and toasting, followed by a two-hour nap, before an agreement was reached. The process was frustratingly slow, though I must admit that the food was often superb.

Travel from Puyang into the surrounding countryside in 1987 was an adventure. The only paved roads at that time were those connecting the city with surrounding county seats. For reasons known only to local planners, all paved roads in the area were being repaired at the same time that sum-

Getting bogged down in the mud and sand on the way to Houhua Village (1987).

mer, eliminating the possibility of unimpeded detour. Traffic was expected to wait patiently until a section of road was completed. Delays of several hours were common. The only recourse was to take unofficial detours through the dirt roads of the villages. In the sand region, those village "roads" are little more than paths that become dust traps when dry, and muddy quagmires when soaked with rain. Four or five times a day our vehicle got bogged down, and we were required to shovel and push. The peasants in the villages were furious as they watched their crops being destroyed and trees broken by detouring traffic. Some put up barriers, and others tried to collect fees from motorists. In one village through which we passed late one night in a heavy downpour the peasants had dug a trench five feet wide and five feet deep across the road. We saw it in time to avert disaster, but for an hour we had to shovel mud in the pouring rain before we could proceed.

On trips that I took into the sand region in subsequent years, the county roads were open, and paving had been extended into some of the larger townships—a manifestation of the rapidly increasing prosperity of the area—but traveling was still slow and dangerous. An unbroken procession of bicycles, donkey carts, trucks, buses, and an occasional car shared the tree-lined main roads with pedestrians, goats, chickens, dogs, and pigs. Vil-

Locals, too, had to push their way through road detours in the sand region south and east of Houhua (1987).

lage people dried their grain on the pavement and sold fruit, vegetables, and handcrafted goods from makeshift stands. The trucks, usually traveling at dangerously high speeds, their horns screaming, were a major hazard. Disaster was inevitable. We witnessed the bloody wreckage of serious accidents almost daily.

The villages, by contrast, were quiet havens from the noise and chaos of the roads. Most of the farming was still labor-intensive, having changed little in that regard in thousands of years. There were few draught animals and very few mechanized vehicles or machinery of any kind. The main crops, wheat, corn, and cotton, were all cut and processed by hand. Most of the surplus was transported to market towns on two-wheeled handcarts. The people were poor, but their living standards were improving. Often their clothes were shabby, but they had enough to eat. Frequently in the past that had not been the case.

I visited a number of villages and interviewed older people who had lived through the years of the Japanese invasion. The names of people and places important to the wartime history of the region soon became familiar to me. One name mentioned especially often was Wang Congwu. He had been

Wang Fucheng, village leader (1994).

among the first Communist Party members in northern Henan and had played an important role in peasant uprisings in that area in the 1920s and 1930s. In trying to learn more about him, I went to his home village, Houhua, for a discussion with his closest relative there, his nephew Wang Fucheng.

From the moment I met Wang Fucheng, he appealed to me as an interview subject. He greeted me with a warmth and enthusiasm that made me feel welcome. That continued each time I visited Houhua Village. He had a wonderful smile that readily gave way to infectious laughter. Underlying his good humor was a self-confident dignity that bore no trace of arrogance. Perhaps because he was illiterate, his recollection of past events was unusually good. He was also remarkably articulate compared to other peasants I have interviewed. As he said in the course of our conversations, "I keep everything in my head, and I work with my mouth."

Another thing that impressed me about Wang Fucheng was his willingness to answer my questions in detail. He was a disarmingly open, frank person who seemed to have nothing to hide. I am inclined to believe his assertion that he could not tell a lie. In that regard, he differed markedly from

Wang Fucheng and Wang Xianghua pictured with the author in the main room of their home. Walls are decorated with calendar art of traditional motifs (1987).

most of the peasants with whom I spoke. The latter tended to be somewhat guarded about what they said to a foreigner, and, not infrequently, I was aware that they were being less than candid. Several times when I questioned Wang Fucheng about politically sensitive matters, he told me that he had nothing to fear from anyone because he had done nothing wrong. That attitude is perhaps naive in light of the multitude of well-documented instances of arbitrary and unjust behavior by Chinese police and other officials,[4] but it is precisely what made Wang Fucheng an effective village leader as well as an ideal informant.

After talking with Wang Fucheng for several days, I decided to change my research project, at least temporarily. I asked him if I could return to Houhua Village in the future to conduct an investigation in which he would be the principal informant and subject. He agreed with enthusiasm and invited me to live in his house when I returned (unfortunately the higher authorities did not allow me to stay with him until my fourth visit, in 1994). He assured me that I could discuss any issue with anyone in the village. Thus, my research came to be concentrated on a single individual and the village in which he lived.

Houhua Village in 1996 is a farming community of approximately 1,400 people. Its population more than doubled during Wang Fucheng's lifetime. Administratively it is subordinate to Liucun Township, a political entity incorporating twenty-two villages with a population of about 25,000 people. Liucun, in turn, is one of twenty townships in Neihuang County. The population of the county approaches 600,000. It is located in the northeast corner of Henan Province, bordering Hebei Province to the north, and only about twenty miles from the western border of Shandong Province. The people and publications of the village, township, and county are the source of most of the information in this book.

It was just over two years before I was able to make a second visit to Houhua Village, in August 1989. I interviewed Wang Fucheng intensively morning and afternoon for two weeks at that time. But I left the village earlier than anticipated because of his poor health. He had suffered a stroke that had paralyzed the right side of his body soon after I had departed in 1987. He could not walk, and although his mind was still sharp, he did not have his former energy. His wife, Wang Xianghua, was worried that reliving the past in such detail was too exciting and too exhausting for him. I agreed.

In May 1990, I visited Houhua Village again for two weeks. On that occasion, I interviewed Wang Fucheng each morning; I spent the afternoons talking with other residents of the village and with township and county officials.

Four more years passed before I returned to Houhua Village. During that time I had been sending Wang Fucheng medicine from the United States for his stroke. His health had improved considerably, and he could walk with the help of a cane. We had corresponded several times each year, and in each letter, dictated to his son or to a retired village schoolteacher, he had urged me to return and to bring my family for a visit. In June 1994 I did so. My wife, daughter, son-in-law, and I arrived in Houhua Village to a very warm and generous reception (which I describe in Chapter 10). My family stayed for only a day, but I returned in July to continue my discussions with Wang Fucheng. I had known him for seven years, and we had become close friends.

Interviews were conducted in the privacy of the home that Wang Fucheng shares with Wang Xianghua. It is a four-room brick structure that had been completed shortly before I arrived in 1987. Typical of most peasant houses in north China, the living quarters face south and form the northern border of a walled courtyard. The only windows are on the south side, facing the sun. A detached kitchen and storeroom are on the east side, and pens for chickens and a dog, as well as a latrine, are on the west side. A heavy iron gate fronting a dirt lane to the south provides the only access to the residence. Just inside the gate is a small raised flower bed backed by a

South side, living quarters and tiled "spirit screen."

moon-shaped "spirit screen" that shields the residence when the gate is open. Beside it grows a Chinese hawthorn tree that provides sweet-smelling, edible blossoms in the spring and welcome shade in the hot summer months. The spirit screen and the framework for the gate are faced with ceramic tiles colorfully painted with birds, flowers, and depictions of traditional gods and heroes. Those aesthetic details, added in 1989, are typical of residences in Houhua Village today, though they would have been ideologically unacceptable in the age of Mao Zedong and an impossible extravagance for even the more prosperous families until the late 1980s. In the past decade almost every family in the village has replaced its mud-brick houses with larger structures made with more durable fired bricks. Although Wang Fucheng's residence is no larger than many others in the village, the house and courtyard are much cleaner and tidier than most.

Wang Fucheng's son, Wang Dejun, lives in an adjacent courtyard to the west with his wife, Li Suzhen, and their three children—a boy, Yanwei (b. 1975), and two girls, Yanxia (b. 1977) and Yongxia (b. 1979). The children, ages twelve, ten, and eight when I arrived in 1987, had become young adults when I visited in 1994. Yanwei had grown over a foot in that time, to about six feet. He had learned to chain-smoke cigarettes, like most of the men in the village, and had taken a job with the township government.

East side, kitchen and storeroom.

West side, latrine, chicken coop, and equipment storage.

Wang Fucheng's gate from the street. Note the absence of tiles on the screen inside the gate (1987).

Yanxia had become a very attractive young woman. She had graduated from junior secondary school and was in a teacher-training academy. Yongxia, always the shyest as well as the most studious of the three, was a budding sixteen-year-old with a self-conscious concern about her clothes and appearance.

When I first began interviewing Wang Fucheng, his grandchildren were frequently nearby, listening with wide-eyed interest to stories they had never heard before. They came home from school for lunch every day and usually ate a bowl of noodles in their grandparents' house, as did I. Yanxia, after overcoming her shyness, would sometimes bring me the text she was using to study English in school and practice her pronunciation. Yongxia and her inseparable friend, Wang Jiping, would spy on us from under beds and behind mosquito nets. Yanwei, the boy, would walk around the village with me, giving me information and introducing me to his neighbors. We became good friends.

Except for family members and the occasional neighbor who would drop in, the only "outsider" present at most of the interviews was Li Rongqing, a young history instructor at Zhengzhou University.[5] He was indispensable for surmounting language hurdles. Wang Fucheng spoke Mandarin, the

From left, Yongxia, Yanwei, and Yanxia (1989).

standard vernacular in China, as do I, but his local accent and village vocabulary were often incomprehensible to me, as was my foreigner's pronunciation to him. When I first went to Houhua Village, Liucun Township officials accompanied me, curious about my intentions, but fortunately they
soon became bored and left us alone, removing any inhibitions caused by
their presence.

As much as possible during the interviews, I wrote in a notebook an
exact translation of Wang Fucheng's words, leaving out only reiteration
and confused responses. Those words constitute the main text of this book.
I refer to our collaborative effort as a "reconstructed autobiography"—
"autobiography" because Wang Fucheng tells his own story; "reconstructed" because I have rearranged his narration. That was necessary because our discussions over the years ranged freely over a variety of topics,
often without regard to chronological sequence. I made every effort in the
process of reconstruction not to distort Wang Fucheng's intended meaning.
I have changed nothing in his account except to add a few clarifying words.

The term "autobiography" requires modification too because Wang
Fucheng told his life story in response to questions that I asked. The interviews were loosely structured. I encouraged Wang Fucheng to reminisce

Village store, with Li Rongqing in foreground (1989).

freely, and I asked him on numerous occasions to discuss anything he felt was important that I had not thought to ask. Usually he preferred a question-and-answer format. Thus, his account of his life was guided significantly by an outsider, albeit one who has spent more than thirty years of his life studying China.

I prepared for my encounters with Wang Fucheng by intensively studying local documents and other materials dealing with village life and with events during the nearly seven decades of his life. In addition, I talked at some length, on several occasions, with officials in Liucun Township and Neihuang County. Township officials generously gave me a copy of the first draft of their recently compiled *Gazetteer* (xiang zhi), the official township record. Such materials are rarely made available to outsiders. The 340 pages of the *Gazetteer* contain what its compilers consider to be the most important information on the history, geography, politics, economics, and cultural affairs of the township and its subordinate villages, and a chronology of major events from 1927 through 1987. I was also allowed to duplicate economic statistics for the township and for Houhua Village for selected years.

In Neihuang town, the county seat, I met with county historians on several occasions and interviewed the county magistrate and other officials.

They gave me completed sections of the new *County Gazetteer* (xian zhi) and drafts of sections still being compiled as well as a copy of the previous *County Gazetteer,* compiled in 1919 and updated in 1937. The contents of those works are similar to but more comprehensive than those of the township records. They fill several volumes. I was also given materials on the history of the Communist Party in Neihuang County, including a particularly useful volume entitled *A Record of Major Events in Neihuang County Communist Party History.* In addition, I gathered similar materials from counties surrounding Neihuang, as well as a number of journal articles and books on regional affairs. Those written materials were supplemented by oral accounts recorded during systematic interviews with members of seventeen households in Houhua Village and by less structured interviews with peasants in a number of other villages and with officials in several counties and townships.

It remains for me to explain the significance of a book on the life of a man who had achieved little distinction outside his own village. In teaching a course on Chinese civilization to university students for many years, I have assigned a book by Ida Pruitt entitled *A Daughter of Han: The Life of a Chinese Working Woman.* Pruitt transcribed the recollections of a neighbor in Beijing as she reminisced about events in her life from 1885 to 1938. At the time of its publication, the book was unique in recording the voice of a working-class person in China. Although it is the account of only one individual's life, it conveys common aspects of Chinese culture more vividly and intimately than is possible in textbooks and academic monographs. It is an excellent vehicle for classroom discussion, and it is very good reading as well. Pruitt's book was an inspiration for this book on Wang Fucheng.

Wang Fucheng's story is significant, too, for its rare microcosmic view of major events in China. Wang Fucheng had lived through an era of great turmoil and change in China. Born during a time of political anarchy in northern Henan Province, he experienced the continuing upheavals of the warlord era, the Nationalist revolution, the rise of the Communist Party, the War of Resistance against Japan, civil war, land reform, and the establishment of the People's Republic. After the Communists came to power, he participated actively in village politics during the campaigns to redistribute the land and collectivize farming in the early 1950s. As village Party secretary from 1954 to 1984, he was in a position both to promote and to modify Communist Party policies that affected the daily lives of the people he led. He played a role in shaping the local implementation of such all-encompassing mass movements as the Great Leap Forward, the Socialist Education Campaign, and the Great Proletarian Cultural Revolution during the era of Mao Zedong, and after Mao died, he presided over the decollectivization of agriculture. His account of the effects of those events on life in one particular village contributes to our understanding of complex movements that swept the whole country. Certainly one of the values of micro-cosmic studies is that they make possible a more accurate and complete picture of the macrocosm. In that regard, the words of an illiterate village cadre can be as illuminating for the historian as those of more famous personalities.

Caveats concerning reliability should be mentioned, though they are obvious to anyone familiar with oral history projects. Wang Fucheng's account is a reconstruction of history shaped, unavoidably, by the limitations of his, and my own, frames of reference, biases, interests, and memories. There is certainly much that Wang Fucheng forgot and probably some things that he misremembered. There are, without doubt, many additional questions I might have asked. It is possible that on occasion Wang Fucheng was prevaricating or intentionally distorting the facts. I am well aware of problems of this nature that other researchers have had when interviewing leaders in rural China.[6] In an effort to gather and to verify information, I carefully reviewed the written record and talked to numerous people in the county, township, and village. My discussions with residents of Houhua Village were limited by the circumstances of my presence there. Everyone was aware that I was a guest in Wang Fucheng's home and that we had become friends. They were unlikely to say anything negative about him in my presence, but I asked them many questions about events and relationships in the village. At no time did their accounts significantly contradict those of Wang Fucheng. I have no doubt that had I stayed in the village longer, a fuller and more complex picture of village affairs would have emerged, but that is largely beside the point. This book is not intended to be primarily an account of Houhua Village; it is, rather, one man's account of his life—an intimate, personal recollection. Therein lies its meaning and value.

Peter J. Seybolt

Acknowledgments

In the seven-year period that I interviewed Wang Fucheng and reconstructed the story of his life, I was assisted by many people, both in China and the United States. I am indebted first of all to Wang Fucheng and his family for their warm and generous hospitality and for their patience in answering the many questions that I asked. At times I must have struck them as naive, obtuse, or excessively nosy, but they were unfailingly gracious and forbearing. I was always made to feel welcome in their home, whether I was sharing meals with them or pressing them to recall details of events from the distant past.

The project would have foundered from the start had it not been for the tireless assistance of Zhengzhou University faculty members Li Rongqing and Han Dongping, both of whom rendered indispensable assistance in coping with village vernacular and providing me with local records and other written materials. They each read the manuscript carefully and offered invaluable advice. Their energy, intelligence, and goodwill made this book possible.

Thanks also to Ralph Thaxton, professor of political science at Brandeis University, for his ingenuity and persistence in making the arrangements with Chinese authorities that first enabled me to visit areas of northern Henan Province that were normally off-limits to foreigners. Thaxton also read the manuscript in an early stage of its development and provided useful insights on the basis of his own extensive experience with village interviews.

Professors Guo Chuanxi and Xu Youli of the History Department of Zhengzhou University made the necessary arrangements with local officials that enabled me to begin my research, and they generously helped me collect written materials from local archives. I benefited from numerous discussions I had with them on matters of mutual interest.

I was given aid, advice, and a number of delicious meals by officials and employees in the offices of Liucun Township and Neihuang County. Without their permission and cooperation, I could not have worked in Houhua Village.

The people of Houhua Village were courteous and polite to the stranger in their midst, and without exception they welcomed me into their homes and answered the many questions that I asked them. I am especially grateful to Wang Dejun, Wang Fucheng's son and successor as village head, and to Wang Changbin, a retired schoolteacher, for their interested assistance over the years.

Anne Chen Paries helped me decipher the handwritten, archaic Chinese of the Wang *Family Register,* which I used extensively in writing the second chapter of this volume.

I have always hoped that the primary audience for this book would be the interested general public and students in university courses on China. I have therefore asked a variety of people to read and comment on the manuscript, including family members, relatives and friends, a succession of students in courses that I teach at the University of Vermont, and a few professional colleagues. In addition to those already mentioned, they include Taylor and Susan Seybolt, Amy and John Tomasi, Gail Bain, Janice Theron, Richard and Harriet Virkstis, Lili Feng, and Rux Martin.

Special thanks are due to my colleague Fred Drake for his help and encouragement; to Stanton Hamlet for drawing the maps of Neihuang County and Liucun Township included in this book; and to Lili Feng for her elegant calligraphy. As always, my most meticulous and best critic has been my wife, Cynthia, who read the manuscript many times and made it significantly more readable. I also thank Susan McEachern, formerly senior editor at Westview Press, Carol Jones, Shena Redmond, and Michelle S. Asakawa for their editorial advice; and the anonymous reader enlisted by Westview for his or her insightful suggestions.

P.J.S.

Weights and Measures

The following conversion table presents a close approximation of the English-language equivalent of traditional Chinese weights and measures used in the text.

Chi   N meter, or 13 inches

Dou   1 decaliter, or 2.54 gallons

Jin   H kilogram, or 1.123 pounds

Li   H kilometer, or N mile

Mu   .0667 hectares, or $\frac{1}{6}$ acre

Qing   6.6667 hectares, or 100 acres

Yuan   a unit of currency

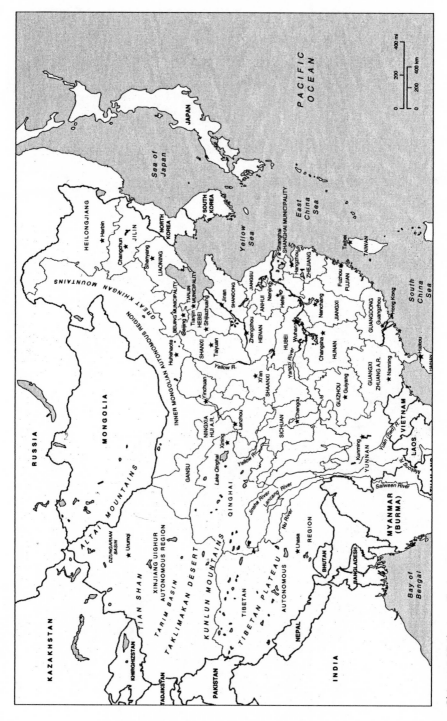

China. * Neihuang County

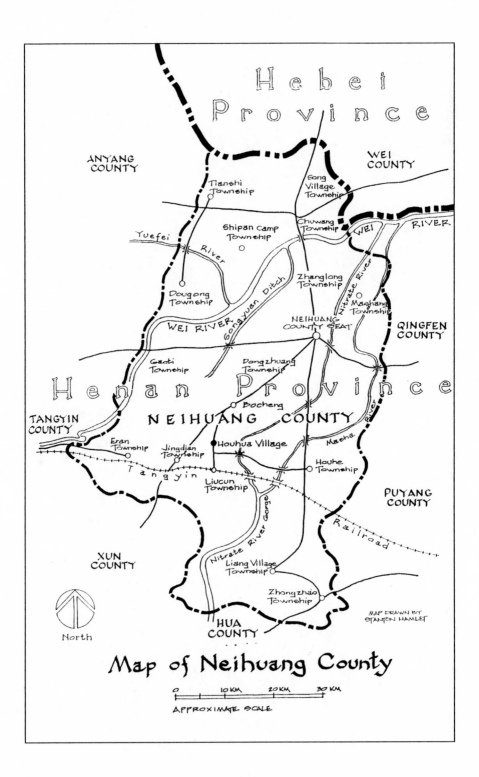

Map of Neihuang County

APPROXIMATE SCALE

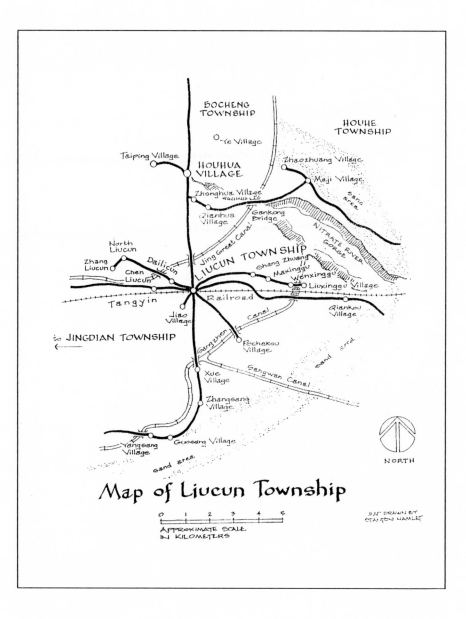

BOCHENG
TOWNSHIP

HOUHE
TOWNSHIP

O-Ye Village

Taiping Village

Zhaozhuang Village

HOUHUA
VILLAGE

Maji Village

Sand
Area

Zhonghua Village

Qianhua
Village

Gankong
Bridge

Jing Great Canal

NITRATE RIVER GORGE

North
Liucun

LIUCUN TOWNSHIP

Zhang
Liucun

Dailicun

Chen
Liucun

Shang Zhuang

Maxinggu

Wenxinggu

Liuxinggu Village

Tangyin

Railroad

Qiankou
Village

Jiao
Village

Canal

→ JINGDIAN TOWNSHIP

Gangzhen

Fachekou
Village

sand area

Xue
Village

Sangwan Canal

Zhangsang
Village

Yangsang
Village

Guosang Village

sand area

NORTH

Map of Liucun Township

0   1   2   3   4   5
APPROXIMATE SCALE
IN KILOMETERS

MAP DRAWN BY
STANTON HAMLET

Throwing the Emperor from His Horse

Introduction:
Houhua Village in Space and Time

People from Under the Stork's Nest:
The Wang Family Comes to Houhua Village

"Our people came from under the stork's nest in the big locust tree" is a common saying in Houhua Village and the surrounding area. According to the *Gazetteer* for Neihuang County, migrants came to Neihuang from Hongtong County in Shanxi Province in the twelfth year of the reign of Emperor Yongle in the Ming Dynasty (A.D. 1414). They had been forced by an imperial edict to move from relatively crowded Shanxi Province to sparsely populated northern Henan Province and settle there permanently as colonists. Records from their place of origin elaborate: Those designated to colonize Neihuang were gathered in the shade of a gigantic locust tree in the courtyard of the Temple of Beneficence in Jia Village, 2 li north of the Hongtong county seat. The ancient temple, built eight hundred years earlier, in A.D. 628, was being used in Emperor Yongle's reign as an administrative office for his emigration officials. The prospective colonists were gathered there before being marched off, leaving ancestors, family, friends—everything they had known—for an uncertain future in northern Henan. As the colonists looked back from a distance, the relatives and friends who had sent them off gradually faded from sight. Finally, the only familiar landmark to be seen was the locust tree with its huge stork's nest. It became a symbol of their former home. The Wang family of Houhua Village was part of that migration.

The circumstances of the Ming Dynasty population transfers that brought the Wang family to Houhua are tragic. During the last years of the Yuan Dynasty (1279–1368), the Neihuang area and much of the rest of the north China plain had been almost entirely depopulated. The Mongol rulers of China at the time were rapidly losing control. Corruption, palace intrigue, factionalism within the bureaucracy, and a breakdown of discipline in the once-vaunted Mongol military organization had rendered the government impotent to deal with a succession of natural disasters in the 1340s. Peasant uprisings were the response. In 1341 alone, over three hundred peasant revolts erupted in Hebei, Henan, Shandong, Hubei, and Hunan provinces. In addition to fighting the Mongols, rebel leaders fought each other for supremacy. The devastation was appalling. Whole provinces suffered serious population depletion. The losses were perhaps heaviest in Henan. For years, battles raged over the north China plain. Neihuang County records state that Mongol troops killed every Han Chinese[1] they saw. The ground was "barren of crops and covered with bodies as far as the eye could see. . . . It had become a land where there were no buildings for the swallows to return to in the spring, the ground was crimson for a thousand li, there were few people and little smoke [from cooking fires]." After years of chaos, the peasant rebel leader Zhu Yuanzhang drove north from the Yangzi–Huai river region. His generals chased the Mongols out of Shandong and Henan and eventually beyond the Great Wall. Northern Henan had been a battlefield for sixteen years.

The victorious Zhu Yuanzhang became Emperor Hongwu, founder of the Ming Dynasty. To put his realm in order, he began forced repopulation of the nine provinces where depletion had been the greatest. Henan received special attention. Sadly, most of those who settled in Neihuang County during Hongwu's reign were either killed or fled the area when Hongwu's death, in 1399, provided the occasion for a murderous four-year war of succession between his nephew, and chosen successor, and his son. The latter won, becoming Emperor Yongle in 1403. Continuing his father's migration policy, Yongle forced many citizens of Shanxi Province to move to the north China plain. In Neihuang and elsewhere, they were organized into colonies consisting of a mix of poor people, vagrants, and convicted criminals. Each household was allotted fifteen to twenty mu of land and relieved of tax obligations for three years. They were protected, ostensibly, by separate colonies of soldiers who farmed 70 to 80 percent of the time and performed garrison duty during the remainder.

The population of Neihuang County more than doubled over the course of the migration. Even so, tax records in the 1460s, fifty years after the people from Hongtong arrived, indicate that the total population was only 14,134. By 1984, it had grown to 568,263, a fortyfold increase in five hundred years. In the same period, the population of all of China had increased between ten- and sixteenfold.

The little that is known of the early history of the Wang family migrants who came to Houhua Village is recorded in their *Family Register*. The names of eighteen generations of males, listed in three large volumes, follow that of their Ming Dynasty founding ancestor Wang Erlao. Like similar family registers throughout China, the record of the Wangs of Houhua contains chapters on proper family names and relationships, burial practices, methods of household protection against fire and thieves, marriage instructions for both males and females, and biographies of family exemplars to provide moral instruction. Unfortunately, there are only twenty-two extant biographies of family exemplars. All lived between 1803 and 1918, the only time the family chronicles recorded the deeds as well as the names of Wang Fucheng's forebears. We learn little about even those few clan members because accounts of their lives conform stereotypically to the values of the Confucian state cult. Virtually all of them were praised for being filial to parents, loyal to family and friends, upright and just in their social relationships, hardworking, frugal, and generous.

Two of the twenty-two biographies exemplify Confucian virtues for women: Gao Jiwen was married to Wang Chunhui, who died at age twenty-nine. She never remarried and remained dutiful to her parents-in-law. She kept her family together and raised her two children despite suffering total destitution when the village was inundated by a flood. To make ends meet she sewed for a living. She is characterized in her epitaph as chaste, filial, and frugal. The other woman is not even named in the biographies but is referred to simply as Wang Cuiling's wife. In addition to "maintaining her virtue" when her husband died and faithfully serving her parents-in-law, she is praised for being kind, feminine, and graceful and for doing her duty without complaint. She raised her children admirably, and "everyone got along well with her."

The Confucian emphasis on education is evident in most of the biographies of Wang family males. It is probable that the great majority of the villagers were illiterate. Certainly that was true at the time of Wang Fucheng's youth. But the exemplars who merited biographies in the clan register, except the two women, were relatively well educated. Seven of them are said to have been promising students who gave up their studies, sacrificing the opportunity for advancement through the civil-service examinations—the main route to prestige, power, and wealth in traditional China—in order to support their impoverished families. Six of those seven then engaged in commercial activities, and one became a teacher. The latter was praised for being so dedicated to education that he moved his school from village to village to avoid the bandit rampages that were endemic in the late nineteenth and early twentieth centuries in Henan Province. Six of the other exemplars were also teachers. Three of them had taken the civil-service examinations many times without success. The most prominent was Wang Yangtong, who as a child had placed first in the Children's Examination (tongshi) in the township and had been sent to a county boarding school fi-

nanced by the state. There he impressed a well-known scholar who spon-
sored his study at an academy in the provincial capital. He became "known
and respected by high officials," but "due to fate" he never passed the
higher-level examinations. He was sought as a teacher by prominent people, but he remained impoverished all his life.

The only recorded member of the Wang clan who brought honor to the
family by passing a higher-level examination was Wang Weisheng. After
many failures he passed the Mingjing (versed in the classics) Examination
at age fifty. That qualified him to sit for the highest degree, the Jinshi (pre-
sented scholar), but he died the same year without ever having been appointed to an official position, "demonstrating how terrible fate can be."

It is possible that another ancestor, Wang Xiaotang, also passed higher-
level examinations, though there is no mention of it in his biography. He
distinguished himself as the only clan member to have become a government official prior to the Communist era. He was county magistrate in
three different places and was then appointed district judge in Guangxi
Province, assistant sub-prefect in Yunnan Province, and, finally, district
magistrate in Yunnan. For his good work he was awarded by the emperor
an honorary blue peacock feather to wear in his cap. In his later years he
returned to his home area and "did much valuable work there" for which
he was recognized with the honorary title *tongxian* (comparable in rank to
the highest degree holder). Two other members of the Wang clan held honorary official titles as well, though neither ever held a position in the imperial bureaucracy.

What the family record tells us, in sum, is that the Wang family of
Houhua had had its moments of distinction but was, for the most part, an
ordinary village family with little to distinguish it from many thousands of
others in the same area.

It is testimony to the Confucian bias of the biographical section of the
Wang *Family Register* that the most famous member of the clan, Wang
Dengbang, is not even included. He was not a scholar; indeed, he remained
illiterate all his life. Nor was he filial to his parents; they died when he was
very young, leaving him an orphan. He lived alone in a temple and begged
for a living until he was discovered and nurtured by the fourth-generation
patriarch of the Plum Flower Boxing School. He became one of the two
most famous martial arts champions in the region and eventually the fifth-
generation patriarch of the Plum Flower style of fighting. His exploits are
recorded in both county and township records. The latter, under the head-
ing "Folk Legends," records popular accounts of his prowess and heroism
in considerable detail.

Wang Dengbang and his friend Yang Bin, from the nearby village of Ding
Zhuang, were trained by the same master. When they fought, neither could
overcome the other, but no one else could come even close to them in abil-

ity. Folk tradition has it that the Kang Xi emperor (1662–1722), before ascending the throne, sought out Wang Dengbang and bowed to him as student to teacher. It is said that he later invited Wang and Yang to come to the capital to serve as "protectors of the nation." Yang accepted and later earned high military rank. Wang, preferring the simple life, feigned illness when invited to court and remained at home, where he gained fame as the scourge of tyrants and bullies. The Kang Xi emperor is alleged to have sent him a pair of lamps with the inscription "Teacher of the Emperor."

When I asked Wang Fucheng about Wang Dengbang, the martial arts champion, and about the exemplars in the *Family Register,* he showed very little interest. His laconic response to my query about Wang Dengbang was, "Oh, he lived 200–300 years ago, he was a famous martial arts fighter. No one compared to him. I know little about what happened in the past." As for the family exemplars, Wang Fucheng said: "In the past the biographies served as models for behavior, but not now. When I was Party secretary we used Communist Party members as our models. The Party did not advocate talking about clan exemplars, so the children today do not know the old stories about family members. I am illiterate, and I don't know them either. You'll have to ask the retired schoolteacher Wang Changbin about that sort of thing."

Although recorded Wang family history seems to have had little influence on Wang Fucheng, recounting it briefly is valuable for putting his life in historic perspective. The man who became the leading official in Houhua Village for thirty years was very much a product of his particular time and place. His achievement would have been unlikely in the past, when education was the key to respect and, often, power. It would have been just as unlikely after his retirement in 1984, when economic and technical knowledge acquired from books began to play an increasingly important role in the rural economy. Wang Fucheng became a powerful person within his own limited world during a time of transition. As an intelligent, energetic, impoverished member of his village, he was exactly the kind of local talent the Communist leadership sought in its efforts to bury the old society and construct a new one. Wang Fucheng owed little to the past and much to the Communist Party. He repaid the Party with loyalty and zeal. But he was loyal to his fellow villagers as well. His main talent was in gaining their confidence and respect, enabling him to lead them relatively peacefully through a period of great upheaval and change. Houhua Village today is a far more prosperous place than it was at any time in the past. It became so as part of a process that has transformed all of China. Wang Fucheng cannot be given full credit for that, but his account of his life makes it apparent that he must be credited for making the pain of transition easier to bear than it was in many villages. To understand the extent of that transition, it is important to look at conditions in Houhua Village in the past.

Legacy of the Yellow River

The names inscribed on maps of Neihuang County reveal significant natural and social characteristics of the area. Places called Flat Plain, Nitrate River, Horse Market, Broken Cart, Three Thousand Mulberry Trees, High Fortress, High Military Colony, Big Stockade, Temple of the High King, and First, Second, and Third Yang Family Villages are indicative of the geography, geology, commerce, silk production, colonization, wars and banditry, religion, and family division of the region. Other local names are evidence of the powerful influence that the mighty Yellow River once had there: High Dike, Golden Dike, Dike Top, Wide Gulch, White Ditch, and Sand Region.

In a less obvious way, the names Neihuang County and Houhua Village both tell of the influence of the Yellow River on their past. Three thousand years ago, the Neihuang (literally "inside yellow") region was a storage area for the floodwaters of the Yellow River. It became a marsh in the first millennium B.C. when the main channel of the Yellow River shifted west, leaving most of the area relatively dry. Han Dynasty (206 B.C.–A.D. 221) records refer to the area variously as yellow ditch, yellow pond, or yellow marsh. This swampy area was surrounded by a dike twenty feet high and almost thirty feet thick after an imperial edict offered the land inside the yellow marsh (i.e., the Neihuang area) to poor people to farm; thus the origin of the name, at least according to some people. Others say that the name refers simply to the location of the county just "inside" the Yellow River. During much of China's early history, the area north of the Yellow River was referred to as *nei* (inside) and south of the river as *wai* (outside). In either case the name Neihuang indicates the significance of the river to the area.

The name Houhua (literally, "rear change") is a reminder of the violent potential of the great river in its frequent change of course. The area now occupied by Houhua Village was once part of a geographically larger village called Kan. In A.D. 993 the shifting waters of "China's Sorrow" obliterated Kan. Eventually, the river moved west, leaving deep gorges and a new river, the Xiao (nitrate). Immigrants later settled three new villages where Kan had been, all appropriately called "Change" (*hua*). Front Change (Qianhua) was in the south, Rear Change (Houhua) was in the north, and Middle Change (Zhonghua) separated them. Though sharing a name, the three Change villages were settled by different lineage groups. Each built a wall defining separate communities. The Wangs settled Houhua, outnumbering the remnants of the He family who were already there.

The legacy of the Yellow River, depicted so vividly in geographic names, significantly shaped the character of the whole region of which Neihuang

County and Houhua Village are a part. Over a period of two thousand years, between the twelfth century B.C. and the twelfth century A.D., the river periodically flowed over parts or all of Neihuang County and Houhua Village, changing its main channel alternately east and west of the county no less than five times. As the giant meandered, it deposited layers of fine silt, many meters thick, over a broad area and left concentrations of salt, nitrate, and alkali where its pooled waters evaporated, assuring poor farming conditions for centuries to come.

The Seven Plagues— Drought, Flood, Wind, Earthquake, Locusts, Salt, and Toxic Chemicals

Although the Yellow River no longer threatened Neihuang when Wang Fucheng's ancestors arrived in the early fifteenth century, it is hard to imagine an environment less hospitable for beginning a new life. Its characteristics are captured in a folk saying common in the area:

> In Spring the land is white with salt
> In Summer floodwaters rush in
> In Autumn locusts fill the air
> In Winter wind kicks up the sand
> In normal years we are cold and hungry
> For only half the year is there enough grain.

The difficulties suggested by this saying are explicitly documented in the *Neihuang County Gazetteer* in a chapter entitled "Good and Bad Fortune." It records events that affected the livelihood of the populace in the county, beginning about a century after the Wang family arrived. The brief entries tell a tale of unrelenting hardship:

1513	Drought. Government sends relief.
1515	Great drought. Much starvation.
1523	Great wind, daylight obscured for over ten days. Drought in summer. Heavy rains in autumn. Starvation.
1524	Drought. Government relief.
1526	Earthquake in twelfth month.
1527	Great drought. Government relief.
1528	Great drought summer and autumn. Decree abolishes 80 percent of taxes. Major government relief.
1530	Great Flood. Taxes reduced 70 percent. Major government relief.

1535   Flying locusts fill the sky.

1536   Spring, great rain and snow in third month. Summer and
            autumn great locust plague. Magistrate Zhang
            Wenfeng makes sacrifices of implements, animals, and
            wine. Locusts disappear. He builds the "Eight Candle
            Temple."

1537   Summer and autumn, great flood.

1543   Great flood. Government relief.

1551   Zhang and Wei rivers overflow, several feet of water
            cover the ground. Much starvation. Government relief.
            Earthquake in eleventh month.

1552   Great flood.

1553   Autumn, great flood.

1555   Earthquake.

1558   A year of unprecedented plenty. Abundant wheat harvest.

1559   Summer, great wind uproots trees, destroys houses and
            buildings.

1561   Locusts, great starvation.

1563   Drought. Insects eat mulberry leaves, no silkworms.

1569   Rivers break their dikes, great flood. Government relief.

1574   Fourth month the sky roars with thunder.

1585   Summer, drought. Government relief, 80 percent of tax is
            canceled.

1586   Summer, drought. Taxes canceled on rice, wheat, and
            stored dates. Shortage of rice. County Magistrate
            Wang Linzhi requests relief rice from the Linde
            storehouse.

1587   Summer, autumn great drought. Famine the next spring.
            County Magistrate Wang again requests relief. 70
            percent of the land tax is canceled.

1588   Spring, disaster. People eat boiled gruel sent in relief.
            Many die of epidemics. County Magistrate Xu
            Chengchu builds the Louze [literally "leaky swamp"]
            Garden to bury the dead.

1590   Third month, third day. Great wind from northwest. Red
            sand blocks the sun. Day is like night. Begins to
            subside after seven hours.

1592   Autumn continuous rain. Zhang and Wei rivers flood,
            destroying fields, crops, and buildings.

1596	Great locust plague. County Magistrate Yen Sizhong requests relief.
1605	Drought.
1607	Great flood. Boats can travel over land.
1608	Great drought. One dou of rice costs 1,000 cash [inflation].
1610	Flying locusts obscure the sun.
1611	Great drought. Land is barren.

In the ninety-nine years of "good and bad fortune" recorded here, there was only one year of good fortune, 1558, but there were thirty-four years of bad. In other words, more than a third of the time there was a disaster of one sort or another, including fourteen droughts, eleven floods, six locust plagues, three earthquakes, three major wind storms, and one major disease epidemic. During one period of fourteen years, 1570–1584, there was nothing more dramatic to report than loud thunder (1574), but then came four successive years of drought, culminating in a major disease epidemic. A special graveyard had to be built to bury the dead. The years that were not mentioned in the record of good and bad fortune were considered "normal"—which in Neihuang County meant subsistence conditions for most of the population.

In the terse entries of the record we do not learn how many people died, how many households were totally wiped out, how many people left the area to beg, how many sold their land and their houses, how many sold themselves into bondage, how many women and children were sold or given away by destitute families, or how many stunted bodies and damaged brains resulted from malnutrition. We can get some impression of the level of misery, however, by looking at the situation in Houhua Village more recently.

In 1942 there was no rain after the spring harvest. Summer and autumn crops could not be planted in the parched ground. By fall, the situation was desperate. Food stores had been exhausted by all but the relatively well-off households. People began to sell their land and leave the area to beg. Some fled to Manchuria to look for employment, as they had often done in the past.

In the fall of 1942, at the height of the drought, swarms of locusts emerged from the banks of the Nitrate River and ate everything in sight, including all of the reeds along the riverbank and the leaves on trees. Drought and locust plague often came together in Neihuang County. From the time the Nitrate River was formed by a Yellow River flood in A.D. 993, the stagnant water in its six-mile back-eddy gulch and the reeds along its banks had provided an ideal breeding ground for locusts. The insects emerged year after year, but every twenty-five to thirty years their numbers were sufficient to cause famine. On such occasions in the past, the county magistrate would lead the people in propitiating prayers. Special places of worship named The Grasshopper Temple (mazha miao) and the Insect King Temple (chongwang miao) were erected for that purpose. In their desperation in 1942 and 1943, the starving people of Neihuang prayed in the temples and assuaged their hunger by drying and eating locusts.

The magnitude of the famine for the residents of Houhua Village is recorded in cold statistics. Of the approximately 800 people resident in Houhua when the drought began, over 15 percent, 125 people, starved to death; 180 of the 200 households, 90 percent of the total, sold their land—which was 80 percent of the total land—and fled the area; 8 percent never returned. Special markets for selling women and female children were established in two nearby market towns and in the Neihuang county seat. Seventy females from fifty households in Houhua Village were sold there or elsewhere. There were even illegal markets for selling human flesh as food in three of the principal market towns in Neihuang County. The drought of 1942–1943 was said to have been the worst in one hundred years. Presumably many of those recorded in the "Record of Good and Bad Fortune" were not as severe, but there is no question that droughts serious enough to be recorded brought great hardship.

Ironically, flooding was almost as common as drought. It was not unusual for both to occur in the same year, when heavy summer rains followed months of dry weather and the accumulating water could not be absorbed by the parched earth. Five rivers run through Neihuang County, all of them subject to periodic flooding. The largest is the Wei, which flows north along the western border of the county and then northeast in the upper third of the county, where it is joined by two other rivers, the Anyang and the Tang, creating a major artery for boat traffic. Until the recent construction of a system of roads, the Wei River was northern Henan Province's principal link with the outside world, connecting it with the Grand Canal and thence the city of Tianjin and the sea. On the eastern side of the county are two other rivers, the Horse Sand River (masha he) and the Nitrate River (xiao he). The latter flows directly through Houhua Village and Neihuang town, the county seat. In addition, just to the northwest of the county lies the tempestuous Zhang River; usually shallow, it becomes a raging torrent during heavy monsoon rains, flooding the border area of northern Henan and southern Hebei provinces.

The worst flood in recent memory was in 1937, when it rained for forty-nine days in succession in July and August. All of the rivers in Neihuang County flooded. In Houhua Village, more than a meter of water covered the ground, destroying houses—many of which were built of mud and straw—and wiping out the crops. In some areas the water level was several times higher. One could travel by boat over a wide area from Xun County, twenty miles south of Neihuang, to Anyang City, twenty miles northwest. Starvation and disease were epidemic. Many villagers temporarily left the area. Bandits rose everywhere, and social chaos ensued. This happened just as the Japanese began their invasion of north China. The flood was a prelude to even greater disaster.

There are no statistics for the 1937 flood comparable to those of the 1942–1943 drought, but some do exist for a more recent flood in 1963. Township records show that in Houhua Village that year all 2,500 mu of agricultural land were flooded by about a meter of water, and 100 houses were destroyed. Neihuang County statistics indicate that 200,000 houses in ninety-three villages were destroyed along with 720,000 mu of crops. No information on deaths is provided other than the terse announcement that "many people and animals were killed." In 1963 the disaster was somewhat ameliorated by government aid, which had not been available in 1937. Airplanes dropped food and other supplies, and boats brought more. The government organized dike repair and channel dredging.

Those customary government relief activities had often been neglected in the past. Toward the end of the nineteenth century, for instance, when the last imperial dynasty was on the verge of collapse, the Zhang River changed its course and flooded two of every three years for several decades—without remedy by the government. Water stood several feet deep in some Neihuang villages until 1921, when the dikes were repaired. Most of the people of the eighteen or so villages most affected by the flood fled, leaving only a few fishermen and reed gatherers. The Zhang River floodwaters did not reach Houhua Village, but the economic and social effects were felt throughout the county and beyond.

The damage done by drought, locusts, and floods to Houhua and surrounding villages was compounded by the fury of wind- and sandstorms. There is a saying in the sand region: "Even if you close the doors tight and paste shut the windows, still you will eat two dou [twenty liters] of sand a year." Another one goes: "In the sand land where there are no trees, wind-blown sand will kill you."

Sand and dust blow every winter throughout north China as the frigid monsoon winds are drawn from central Asia toward the sea. The velocity of the wind often increases as it funnels through the broad pass where Neihuang County is located, between Shanxi (western mountains) and Shandong (eastern mountains) provinces. When the winter dust storms reach gale proportions every several years, the fine grit once deposited by the Yellow River rises in great clouds obscuring the sun for hours and sometimes days. Until the mid-1960s, such winds would destroy crops, blow down houses, and bury whole villages. Even in normal years the destruction was formidable. As late as the 1950s approximately 100,000 mu of winter wheat, about one-sixth of the total for Neihuang County, was destroyed annually by wind-driven sand.

Villages on the west bank of the Nitrate River in what is known as the "flying sand region" were continually destroyed and partially buried by sand. Just as the Yellow River had divided Kan Village into the three Hua Villages, wind-blown sand ridges divided Yang Village into Greater Yang, Second Yang, and Third Yang villages. At the Temple of the High King, built during the Tang Dynasty (A.D. 618–906), tombs located behind it were long ago deeply buried by a huge mound of sand. Blown by winds in the early twentieth century, the sand now forms a ridge over three miles long. There are numerous places in Neihuang County where inscribed stele memorialize the damage caused by great sandstorms. Houhua Village was never completely buried by wind-blown sand, as were some of its neighbors, but damage was continual and often serious. Until recently, wind-blown sand was a major cause of arguments, fights, and killings throughout the sand region as farmers erected barriers to redirect calamity from their land to their neighbors'. Sand-area farmers have always tried to plant trees and other wind-barrier vegetation, but this was not done systematically, or very effectively, until the mid-1960s.

Yet another plague to test the endurance of the people of Houhua and surrounding villages was the continuing accumulation of mineral deposits, especially salt, nitrate, and alkali. The greatest cause of this phenomenon was evaporation of Yellow River water a millennium ago, but new deposits were laid down annually thereafter as floodwaters overflowed the Nitrate River ditch and gradually evaporated during the dry seasons in winter and spring. The floodwaters also raised the water table, normally 8–10 meters deep in Houhua, bringing minerals to the surface.

Where the minerals were most abundant, farming was poor or impossible. The poorest villages in the sand region, many of which stood along the west bank of the Nitrate River, were those with the heaviest mineral deposits. In some villages it was impossible to grow crops. Inhabitants eked out a meager subsistence by sun-drying "small salt," scraping surface nitrates, and decocting alkali. In this desperately poor area the houses were mostly broken-down reed structures. None but the most impoverished families would consider marrying their daughters into the "salt-land villages." It was a land of many bachelors and a breeding ground for banditry.

Houhua Village was better off than some of its neighbors—Horse Driver, Dragon Village, High Temple, Zhang Village—but over one-third of its agricultural land, 1,500 mu of a total of 4,000 mu, was so salt-encrusted that it was until recently nearly worthless for farming. Even land in which the minerals were not so concentrated was not very fertile. Most of the peasants in Houhua and hundreds of other villages in the old course of the

Yellow River supplemented their agricultural income by making and selling salt and other minerals. So important was it to their income that state-government attempts to eliminate salt production in the sand region, in the interest of the officially licensed salt industry in Tianjin City, led to massive popular revolts in 1915 and 1932, forcing the government on both occasions to back down. But as important as salt was to the local economy, the salt lands produced but a fraction of the income generated by crops. Mineral deposits were as much a cause of misery as were floods, droughts, and locusts.

Another product of the local geology that contributed to the misery of the populace was a large concentration of fluoride in the water. That chemical, often artificially added to water supplies in Western cities to protect children's teeth, was present naturally in sufficient quantities to destroy the teeth, bend the bones, and dwarf the bodies of the people in Houhua. In Liucun Township, eighteen of its twenty-two villages had serious fluoride problems; Houhua Village was among the worst. An investigation in the Township in 1981 revealed that over 80 percent of the population of Houhua suffered serious effects of fluoride poisoning. Manifestations ranged from hardened brown teeth to bowed backs, shrunken limbs, incapacitation, and early death. Even after it became known that flouride in the water was to blame, not much could be done about it; the technology to drill deep tube wells and draw the water with electric pumps was not available. When the problem was finally addressed effectively in Houhua in 1983, engineers had to drill 300 meters to reach safe drinking water.

In sum, nature has not been very kind to those who inhabit Houhua and other villages in Neihuang County. Victims of drought, flood, earthquakes, locusts, sand, salt, and toxic chemicals, the residents constantly have had to fight for their survival. But in the past half century, the situation has been ameliorated to an extent unimaginable to Wang Fucheng's forebears. The effects of drought have been almost eliminated by irrigating with well and river water drawn by electric pumps. Danger of flood has been greatly reduced in the process as river water has been pumped and rechanneled. Dredging, draining ditches, and building strong dikes have given added protection. Irrigation has lowered the water table and thus the salt and alkalinity level in the soil. Minerals on the surface have been largely washed away by ditching, mounding, and leaching techniques, or removed by planting salt-absorbing vegetation. Wind-blown sand is restrained by millions of strategically planted trees and by crops sown in sand areas now devoid of salt. Locusts are controlled by insecticide.

The comparative prosperity of Houhua Village today has been enhanced as well by the introduction of chemical fertilizer and hybrid seeds. Land that once had an average yield of 24 jin per mu now averages 500 and occasionally reaches 800. The relative isolation imposed on Neihuang County

Street outside Wang Fucheng's gate. Boy at left is Yanwei (1987).

in the past by the unpredictable Wei River has been alleviated by long bridges that enable traffic to cross five times faster than was possible on the ferry boats traditionally used. Paved roads now link the county towns formerly connected by dirt paths that frequently were all but impassable.

These benefits did not come without accompanying problems. The population has grown enormously, threatening to outstrip productive capacity and jeopardize recently achieved prosperity. The average amount of cultivated land per person fell from 3.44 mu in 1949 to 1.57 mu in 1987. As noted earlier, roads are jammed with people and vehicles, and highway slaughter is epidemic as trucks weave at breakneck speed through an obstacle course of donkey carts, bicycles, and pedestrians. Intensive production threatens to exhaust the soil, and fertilizers and insecticides portend long-term damage to the ecology. The government, which played a major role in improving conditions in the area, has now become a major burden itself. Not only did it interfere, as never before, in all aspects of people's lives in the process of transforming the area, but it has since become a huge and parasitic bureaucracy that, peasants commonly complain, takes more than it gives.

Jingdian market town.

Nevertheless, government today is preferable by far to the political chaos that reigned during Wang Fucheng's youth and in the years prior to his birth. A brief account of the politics of that earlier era will help explain the persistence of natural disasters and the growth of the revolutionary movement in which Wang Fucheng was to play an important role in his village.

The Eighth Plague—Political Chaos

From the beginning of the twentieth century until 1949, the central government of China, in its various forms, exercised little control over Neihuang County. The imperial government of the Qing Dynasty (1644–1911) was unable to implement its policies in northern Henan Province in its waning years, and the Republic, which succeeded the Qing in 1912, was no more effective. Following the death of President Yuan Shikai in 1916, successive "national governments" presided in the capital, Beijing, but real power had devolved to provincial military governors and regional warlords. Between 1916 and 1928, northern Henan was dominated at different times by the armies of four different warlords.[2] Their changing alliances and antagonisms, punctuated by treachery and violence, created an environment in which high taxes, forced military recruitment, and loss of life and property were endemic.

During the years of warlord turmoil, the configuration of power at the local level changed significantly. Bandit gangs rose in profusion, and they in turn were confronted by locally organized militia and by secret religious societies known collectively as Red Spears. According to the 1937 *Neihuang County Gazetteer*, in the 391 villages in the county, almost no family of middle income or above had escaped the depredations of bandits. People were robbed outright or held for ransom; "no one was safe day or night." The poor, who had nothing to rob, suffered as well. They were innocent victims of bandit violence, bandit gang members themselves, or recruits in local militia and protective societies. Mentioning only the worst bandit incidents in the early 1920s, the *County Gazetteer* records 30 deaths and 140 kidnap victims in one raid on a single village; 108 deaths in another; 300 killed or wounded in another; and 1,000 buildings burned, 100 people kidnapped, and 70 killed or wounded in yet another. As Wang Fucheng recounts later in this book, 80 people in Houhua Village were killed as a result of two bandit gangs raiding the village and fighting each other when the Japanese army first arrived in 1938.

The civil militia and religious societies organized to combat warlord and bandit exploitation were somewhat effective in their stipulated duty, but they often became exploiters of the common people themselves. In 1926, village and township militia, which had for centuries been organized in times of need in China, began to be systematically united into district units in Neihuang County. Any group of villages that could gather together at least forty guns became a guard unit with a director and a company commander. Twenty of these units were organized throughout the county, incorporating about twenty villages each. All were coordinated and directed by a central guard unit in the county seat. They guarded against bandits, but invariably they were under the control of relatively wealthy people and served their interests by enforcing the collection of rent payments and taxes. Locally levied supplementary taxes on land in Neihuang County doubled in 1928 (from 2.5 yuan to 5 yuan per mu), and tax silver was collected three years in advance. The militia was a principal beneficiary of the tax as well as principal agent to enforce payment. Popular discontent with the self-serving activities of the militia leaders is apparent in the success that the Communists had—when they became active in the area in 1928—in rallying mass support by attacking militia commanders and their wealthy patrons. Wang Fucheng recounts one such incident in detail while discussing the early years of his life.

The secret religious societies were dominated by relatively prosperous families as well. The Sacred Way Society, the most powerful such association in Neihuang County, was organized and led by Wei Liuhe, head of one of the seven families in the county who owned 10,000 mu or more of land. The average amount of land per capita in the county at the time was about 3.4 mu per person. Another organization, the Gate of Heaven Society, that operated in parts of Neihuang and counties to the west of it was led by Yang Guanyi, a wealthy merchant and landowner. Like the militia, the religious societies could be both protectors and predators, depending on circumstances at any particular time. In Wang Fucheng's opinion, "Their purpose was to get power . . . then they could be like kings and collect crops and money from the people."

The chaotic political situation in northern Henan began to change in 1928, when the new Nationalist Party (Guomindang) defeated, or reached accommodation with, the warlord armies and began to establish a new order. In the next several years, it reorganized the militia, greatly increased police forces, and reached a modus vivendi with the powerful leaders of religious societies. The problem for the common people was that Guomindang measures designed to improve local security and well-being were very expensive. Taxes steadily increased—especially local, supplementary taxes for things like education, construction, local government, police, and militia. By the mid-1930s such taxes were ten times what they had been at the beginning of the Republican era (1912) and exceeded the regular land and head taxes, traditionally the main source of revenue, by two to three times. It is impossible to determine how heavy the tax load was for the average peasant, but even the official *County Gazetteer* lamented "the heavy tax burden on the people." In submarginal farming regions like Neihuang County, any tax was hard to bear. Increasing taxes provoked increasing discontent.

All of these conditions provided fertile ground for cultivating a Communist movement in northern Henan Province. Wang Fucheng's uncle, Wang Congwu, was one of the first people in the central plains area of China to join the Communist Party. He did so in 1927, when he was only sixteen and a student in a secondary school in Daming City. He and other young activists returned to their villages and were fairly effective in leading tax revolts and mobilizing people to attack local bullies. In 1931 and 1932 he was a leader of a successful rebellion of thousands of local salt makers protesting a government ban on local salt-making operations in the interest of big monopoly salt enterprises on the coast. The Communist movement gained momentum after that, but only briefly. The Nationalist Party, which did not even have a party branch in Neihuang County until 1931 and which had little effective control over local power holders in Neihuang until 1935, was increasingly effective in the following two years, particularly in its "Communist annihilation" campaign. By mid-1936, Wang Congwu was in jail, and many of his comrades had been killed or had become inactive. It seemed that the national government in Nanjing was on the verge of establishing a degree of unity and order not seen in Neihuang for many decades.

Then, in 1937, the Japanese attacked, initiating World War II in China and re-creating chaos in the central plains for another eight years. Four years of civil war between the Communists and the Nationalists followed Japanese surrender in 1945. Not until 1949, with the establishment of the People's Republic of China, would there be relative peace and order. The political chaos characteristic of the first quarter-century of Wang Fucheng's life would influence deeply his mentality and his career as village leader.

1

Poverty, Bandits, and Japanese Invaders: Early Life, 1923–1946

My discussions with Wang Fucheng began at the beginning, with his memories of the early years of his life. We discussed his family, their living conditions, the two villages in which he lived, customs, religious beliefs, and holidays. I asked him to recall the happiest and unhappiest times of his youth and to describe the effects of major events such as the famine of 1942, the Japanese invasion and occupation of northern Henan Province, and the rise of the Communist Party in the area. Information about these things had to be drawn from the recesses of Wang Fucheng's memory little by little. Much of it he had not thought about in a long time. His wife, Wang Xianghua, listened with interest, occasionally putting in a word. She reminded him, for instance, that when he was young he was so obscure and insignificant that no one knew his name. Occasionally Wang Fucheng would call in others, like his friend Wang Changmin, to help refresh his memory. Other villagers would drop in too, partly out of curiosity about the foreigner in their midst, and would frequently offer their comments. Eventually, Wang Fucheng had to close his gate to control the crowd.

Wang Fucheng was animated during our early talks. He enjoyed recalling the past, even though much of it had been characterized by bitter poverty and deprivation. He often laughed and slapped his knee in mock disbelief as he recalled how poor he and his family had been. He became very grave, however, as did all of the people I interviewed in northern Henan villages, when discussing the famine of 1942–1943. His friend Wang Changmin broke down and cried and had to leave the room for several minutes when he recalled how his parents had starved to death during that catastrophe forty-five years earlier.

When I inquired about the war years, 1937–1945, the peasants in many villages where I conducted interviews referred to the Japanese reflexively as guizi (devils). That was not the case with Wang Fucheng. Rarely did he use deprecating terms when discussing others, a forbearance that characterized his personality. He was, however, utterly disdainful of the bandits, the leaders of secret religious sects, and various collaborators with the Japanese who preyed on the people under Japanese auspices during the war years. There were no Robin Hoods among them in Wang's mind, and no redeeming character traits. Clearly the Communists were Wang Fucheng's heroes, though he spoke of their activities unemotionally, taking for granted the rectitude of the role that they played in transforming his world. That attitude is easy to understand as he recalls the first twenty-three years of his life in this chapter.

Throughout this book, I have tried to maintain on the written page the cadence of Wang Fucheng's speech as well as his vocabulary. His remarks were usually short and to the point. The transcribed sentences are, accordingly, succinct and terse. They reflect Wang Fucheng's characteristic no-nonsense pragmatism, though they tend to mask the warmth and generosity of his personality.

Wang Fucheng:

I was born in this village sixty-seven years ago. My father was a farmer and salt maker. We were very poor. I was the youngest of four children, two boys and two girls. First sister was twelve or thirteen years older than I, second sister was seven or eight years older, and my brother was three years older.

When I was six years old, my father died. At that time, he smoked a white powder [opium or morphine] that had been brought to China by foreigners. Five or six people in this village smoked it. My father was very poor and had to steal to buy it. He stole from one of my uncles and was killed by him. I think he was buried without a coffin in the family grave plot. I don't remember. He was only in his thirties.

Before my father started smoking opium, our family was fairly well-off compared to many others. My grandfather had divided his property among his four sons, and my father's portion was eight to ten mu of land [6 mu = 1 acre] and a three-room house. The house was made of mud bricks, but it had a tile roof, which was fairly unusual here. Most houses had roofs made of sorghum stalks. Only a few comparatively rich families had houses made from kiln-fired bricks and with tile roofs. The farmland my father inherited was of poor quality, but it was enough to support us. Then, because of his drug addition, my father gradually sold all of the land except the two mu where the family grave plots were. He also sold the house with the tile roof and built a two-room mud house with stalks on the roof. Eventually he no longer worked, and my mother, sisters, and brother and I had to beg from our relatives to survive.

After my father was killed, my mother took me to live with my grandfather and grandmother in Jiang Village, six li [3 li = 1 mile] from here. I lived there until 1946, when I was twenty-three. When I returned to Houhua, I knew no one.

The family broke up after my father died. My brother went to Shanxi Province as a long-term laborer and later was conscripted as a soldier by the Warlord Yen Xishan.[1] He was killed by the Japanese during the War of Resistance [1937–1945]. My two sisters were married and went to other villages. They were introduced to their husband's families by relatives. There was no special marriage ceremony. We were too poor. They just went to live with a man's family and were considered married. Actually, my older sister had three husbands at different times. She had a very hot temper and left when her husbands beat her. She had nothing to eat, so she had to go to another man.

Both of my sisters had bound feet, as did most of the women around here, some until the late 1940s. There was an old saying: "big feet, loss of face." I remember the ribbons binding my sisters' feet. My sisters mostly stayed at home. If they went out on the street, the village people would laugh at them and look down on them for being out. Because women with bound feet could do no farm work, those in the poorest families didn't bind their daughters' feet. The first concern was survival. But, I would say that about 80 percent of the women here had bound feet even though Houhua was a very poor village. It was difficult for my sisters to walk. It took my older sister over an hour to walk three li to Taiping Village, where her second husband's family lived. It is a twenty minute walk for me. My older sister died of a large tumor when she was forty-six or forty-seven years old.

After my mother took me to live in Jiang Village with her parents, our life was very difficult. My grandfather had lost his sight because he was old and had overworked. He had the white eye disease [cataracts]. My mother was deaf. She had been ill when she was young and couldn't hear after that. We had about six mu of poor land, enough to feed us for only about half a year. We had no meat and rarely ate vegetables. Every year we ate sorghum porridge twice a day until it ran out, then we ate tree leaves, grasses, roots, and wild vegetables. I did not eat a *mantou* (steamed wheat bun) until I was seventeen or eighteen years old. I was always hungry. I never went to school. Having nothing to eat, how could I study? To this day I cannot read or write. Later, when I was Communist Party secretary of Houhua Village for thirty years, I did everything by memory. I kept everything in my head.

In Jiang Village my mother helped support us by weaving cotton cloth. Someone would take it to market and buy more raw cotton for her to weave. Our clothes were made from the cloth she wove, as were our cotton shoes, which were dyed with red soil. We never had much to wear. We couldn't even afford a long overcoat for winter, so I wore a short cotton-filled jacket with a belt around the waist. Even when I was twenty years old my mother and I had to share a single quilt when we slept.

I collected firewood to sell. I remember being beaten when collecting wood near the property of a rich family. They thought I was stealing. Sometimes I did steal. Once I stole about 100 jin [1 jin = 1.1 lbs.] of leaves from pear trees. We boiled them and ate them for quite a long time. When I was sixteen or seventeen I collected manure for fertilizer. One day when two of us were collecting manure, we were accused of stealing and told to eat it. The other person did, but I didn't because my grandfather came in time.

I sometimes worked as a short-term laborer for the more prosperous households in the village. I was used only for a few days at harvest time to cut corn and sorghum. I received no pay but was given my food for the day. I remember well that when I was about eighteen I was working for a rich peasant and was given five steamed wheat buns at noon and four more in the evening. They were the best thing I had ever eaten, and that was the first time I had ever had enough to eat. The next day there was no work, and I was hungry again.

There were only about four or five rich peasants in Jiang Village, and no landlords. Almost everyone there was poor. We were no poorer than many others.

I had no knowledge of the world at that time. I never traveled far from the village, even to a nearby market town. The main market was Jingdian, eight li from here. I had no money and nothing to trade, so why should I go? I was too hungry. No money. I didn't even have friends when I was a child. Everyone ignored me. People didn't know my name. They just called me Er Wang Xiao (Little Second Wang).

Because of my poor diet I was always sick. That is why I am so short. I often had diarrhea, but I never saw a doctor. How could I? I had no money. There were no doctors in our village. When rich people got sick they called in a doctor from 10 to 20 li away. Doctors wouldn't treat sick people until they had been given a banquet. They would first eat and drink and receive gifts. Ordinary people couldn't afford that. We did have a spirit medium in the village who claimed to cure people with magic spells and by contacting the spirits of the dead, but that was just superstition.

In those days, of one hundred children who were born, eighty wouldn't grow up. An uncle of mine had four sons, all of whom died. Only a daughter was left. She now works far from here. In those days few people lived to be sixty. Today many are in their seventies and eighties.

The best times were festival days, especially the New Year celebration, what we call Spring Festival today. We would mix sorghum flour with pieces of dried sweet potato to make a steamed bun. This was our main food for the holiday, but we also made a larger steamed bun, called *huazi*, of wheat flour and the pulp of sweet potato after the juice had been pressed out. We put Chinese dates on top of it. We offered it as a sacrifice to the gods, then we ate it.

Another special day was the Moon Festival in the middle of the eighth month of the old [lunar] calendar. People who could afford it bought moon cakes to eat. We just made a steamed bun with corn flour and put turnip in it.

In the spring at the Clear Bright Festival (Qing-Ming) people burned paper for their ancestors. We ate no special food at that festival. It was a time to sweep graves and repair tombs. The Wang family tombs of many generations are in Houhua Village, but I never went back there at that time.

There were seven or more temples in Jiang Village and over ten in Houhua Village. Some were longer than this house, and some were as small as a mat. I remember the names of only some of them. In Jiang there was the Goddess of Mercy Temple, the Bodhissatva Temple, the Old Mother Temple, and the Buddha Temple. In Houhua there was the Old Grandfather Temple, also called the Temple of the Jade Emperor Supreme God; the Fire Star Temple; the Bodhisattva Temple; the Old Grandmother Temple; and the God of War Temple.

The Grandfather Temple, in the west of Houhua Village, was the largest. It had a big Buddha statue in the middle, six big statues on either side, and dozens of other statues. I don't know who built those temples or where the money came from. Some were hundreds of years old. I suppose that many families donated money, especially families of people who got sick.

When I was a child I did kowtow to gods in the temples, but I never believed in it. I just followed others. We had pictures of gods in our house, and we kowtowed and burned incense in a bowl when unusual things happened or when we ran short of something. We had pictures of the grandfather god, the god of wealth, and the stove god. I seldom bowed to them, but the old women of the house did. When I was older, after the war with Japan, I helped smash the temples and the statues. The temple bricks were then given to retired soldiers for building houses. There were three or four households of Christians in most of the villages around here. There are still two old women in this village who have those beliefs, and in Jingdian market town there is a Catholic priest. I don't know much about that religion. None of the gods were useful for solving real problems.

The worst time I can remember was the great famine of 1942. It rained some in the spring of that year, but then it was completely dry for three planting seasons. The crops all died. During the summer of 1942, 80 percent of the people of Jiang Village and Houhua left home to beg. Most went to Shanxi Province; some went to Shandong Province and the northeast (Manchuria). Many never returned. One or two hundred people from Houhua either never returned or starved to death. More starved in Houhua than in Jiang Village. Many young children, especially girls, were sold at that time. A girl cousin of mine who was twelve years old was sold to a stranger for seven or eight dou [decaliters] of grain. Another uncle sold both his daughters. Some people gave away their children just to save them from starving. People tried to sell their property and their children to relatives. Those who bought them were not necessarily rich. The price was very low. It makes me very sad to discuss those times. It was a sorrowful period of our history. We had to sell my grandfather's house, where we lived, to a family named Su from Jiang Village. It was a three-room brick house. We got only eight dou of grain for it. We then built a very simple mud house with sorghum stalks on the roof. When it rained, water poured through the roof, making mud of the floor. We also had to sell our six mu of land, all we had. From then on we had to rely on relatives. Some lived ten li from Jiang Village. I went there to ask for grain. I also collected manure and firewood and traded them for grain.

The government didn't help at all during the famine. It was a time of great confusion. Before the Japanese came [in 1938] the villages here were administered by a village head, also called a guarantor head, who was responsible for all village affairs, especially tax collection. He was assisted by several section heads in charge of about thirty households each. The village head reported to a big guarantor head who was responsible for taxes and keeping order in several villages. He reported to the county government. No one wanted to be the village head because he could get in trouble and even be beaten by higher authorities if he couldn't collect enough tax money. Usually the landlords and rich peasants paid poor people to act as village head. They often chose unemployed loafers who were glad to be paid something to do the job. The village head changed often, every two years or so. I recall a man called Er Huai Ye (secondary evil lord) was village head at one time. That is what we called him because he was so cruel, but his real name was Wang Yintang.

Taxes were paid in silver and copper money based on the amount and value of your land. We got the money by selling our products at the market. If a family could not or would not pay, the family head might be taken to jail by the armed county police and beaten badly. I remember a family named Liu who couldn't pay their tax even though they sold their land. Just before New Year's Festival, when all debts are due, he was beaten severely with a stick. They beat him forty strokes, and he promised to pay, but later he just couldn't and they left him alone. Actually, often there was no fixed tax standard and no fixed time for collection. They just called for taxes when they wanted them, usually after the harvest. Sometimes bandits also came and made us pay.

There were a number of bandits in this area at that time. Before the Japanese arrived, they usually came in small groups, though there were some large bandit gangs of several hundred people. I remember that there was one near the Yu River area, about seventy or eighty li north of here, led by He Jiuxiang. His gang was fighting another one in Houhua Village when the Japanese first came in 1938. In those days the Nationalist (Guomindang) government didn't care if the bandits fought each other or not. When bandits came to plunder, resistance was organized by secret religious societies (*huidaomen*), not by the government.

Ding Shuben was the government magistrate in Puyang County when the Japanese arrived. Jiang Kaishek told his troops not to resist, so Ding and his men withdrew and there was no local government.[2] There was no formal Guomindang government in this area from 1938 to 1945. Many bandits came out then, and many more secret religious societies with superstitious beliefs were formed. They burned incense, kowtowed, and chanted, thinking that knives and bullets would not then hurt them. I don't know all the details, but their purpose was to get power. They got recruits by giving food and clothing and protecting families. They were out to control several hundred villages; then they could be like kings and collect crops and money from the people. Many of them joined the Japanese when they came, and some joined the Central Government Army. They differed from ordinary bandits in that the latter had no superstitious beliefs. Ordinary bandits joined with others like themselves to control an area, acting like evil tyrants. Both types of bandits killed a lot of people and stole crops. They were very cruel.

A religious-society leader named Sun Buyue controlled most of the villages in Xun and Hua counties just south of here. I remember when someone from this area traveled to Xun County and was caught by Sun. He was put on a board and had nails driven through his hands and feet. Two other people I know of were captured there and starved to death.

Most of the area north of here was controlled during the war by the Imperial Assistance Army stationed in Anyang, Tangyin, and Wei counties. They were Chinese traitors who collaborated with the Japanese. We called them "Japanese running dogs." Many were former Nationalist troops. Jiang Village and twenty or thirty others were controlled by Li Ying, a former Nationalist officer who went over to the Japanese. He had his own organization, which he called the "Cleanse the Countryside Bureau." His purpose, too, was to seize power for himself. He had about a thousand soldiers under him—his own troops, loyal to him personally—but they were backed by Japanese soldiers in Dongzhuang, a market town about ten li from here. He established various branch bureaus that controlled ten to twenty villages. Jiang Village, where I lived, was under his control throughout the war. The Cleanse the Countryside Bureaus became like police stations to keep order, but the situation was very chaotic nevertheless. There were many armed forces that came any time they wanted, and we were left impoverished. The poor had nothing to give, but the middle families had no way out, so they had to give. Some of the rich families, like that of Wang Wei in Xinzhuang Village, had a relationship with the bandits. He had about ten qing of land (about 1,000 acres) and twenty or thirty armed men of his own, but he still had to pay off the bandits, and when the (Communist) guerrillas came and asked for supplies, he had to pay them, too.

Early Communist Party Activities

The area from Houhua Village east to Yanggu, about twenty-five li away, was the old Communist base area where the guerrillas were strongest. Houhua and Qiankou villages and Jingdian market town were the center of Communist activities when they first began here [in the late 1920s]. My uncle Wang Congwu and my cousin Wang Zhuoru were among the first people in this area to join the Communist Party. They both are now high officials and live in Beijing. Wang Congwu is retired vice secretary of the Central Disciplinary Committee, and Wang Zhuoru is vice director of the Main Office of the Supply and Sales Cooperative. Wang Congwu was born in this village (Houhua) in 1910. My father was his older brother. There were six children in my grandfather's family, four boys and two girls. Only Wang Congwu was sent to school. My grandfather couldn't afford to send the others. They remained illiterate all their lives except for number-four uncle, who became literate enough to write simple letters after Wang Congwu got him a low-level cadre job at the Beijing railway station in the 1950s.

Congwu was intelligent and clever. He had many friends and was a natural leader. He attended an old-style private school in this village and then went to Kaizhou [the former name of Puyang, then the county seat] when he was about nine years old. He was able to go away to school because he was engaged that year to be married. His prospective father-in-law, a rich peasant from Horse Market Village, about eight li from here, paid for his schooling. Later he went to a secondary school in Daming City for a few months. He joined the Communist Party in 1927 when he was only sixteen years old. He and Wang Zhuoru, who joined when he was fifteen, began to mobilize the masses to struggle against the landlords. My friend Wang Changmin, who was here at the time, can tell you more about it.

Wang Changmin:
They organized a peasant association, which most of the poor peasants joined, and started a peasants' night school in Houhua. It had over fifty students. Similar schools were started in Qiankou Village nearby and in Jingdian market town. The first three Communist Party branches in this area were formed around these schools. The Communist Party was a secret or-

Wang Fucheng standing in front of the 1928 peasant association headquarters (1987).

ganization at that time. There were about eight members here in Houhua, including three women. They did a lot of propaganda work, urging the poor to form peasant associations and to rise up and settle accounts with landlords. They organized the hired laborers to demand more money from the landlords and threatened to go on strike if they didn't get satisfaction. They wanted the landlords to tell publicly how much interest they made on loans and how much land they took. This was happening in many villages. In early 1928 there was a peasant uprising in Houhua, Qiankou, and about ten other villages in this area. Over a thousand peasant association members went to Wenxinggu Village to settle accounts with Cai Hongbin, a big, evil landlord and the head of the landlords' united village militia. They were successful, and the struggle spread. Later there was a big meeting in Wenxinggu Village to celebrate the victory. Landlord militia, led by a man named Du Jingsheng, attacked the meeting. A number of people were killed and injured. Some Communist Party members, including Wang Fucheng's cousin, Wang Zhuoru, were arrested. Wang Congwu escaped. The next day, Du Jingsheng's landlord militia came to Houhua Village and fought the whole day. Du lived in this village, and peasant association members here had taken his wife prisoner. The peasant association members had no rifles, only bird guns. There was a wall around the village then, and they were able to keep the militia out, but five of the peasant association members were killed, including three Communist Party members. The battle stopped when a rich peasant, Wang Yinzhen, mediated between the two sides. The militia then entered the village and took away the bird guns. Many peasant association members fled to other villages.

Later, peasant association members went to Puyang to petition the Guomindang government because at that time it had some Communist Party members in it who would be sympathetic. The government arrested the landlord militia leader Du Jingsheng. He died in jail three years later.

Wang Fucheng continues:

After the Wenxinggu incident, there was not much Communist activity in this village until 1937, when the war with Japan began. There were only about eight Party members. Three of them, Zhao Lanzhi, Wang Shanlan, and Sun Qiumei, were women. One Party member, Wang Debin, later became a traitor to the Japanese. Party members at that time did mostly underground work, such as organizing peasants to oppose giving grain to the landlords after the harvest. They had successes and failures. The landlords had guns.

My uncle Wang Congwu replaced Zhao Jibin as Party secretary for Puyang County after the Wenxinggu incident. He led a big uprising of thousands of salt makers in 1931 and 1932 against the salt police from Tianjin who were sent to enforce a new government salt monopoly. Everyone here supported the salt makers' uprising, but only seven or eight people joined the demonstrations. We were on the edge of the salt-making district. After the salt makers' victory there were several days of opera performances to show the local people the authority of the salt makers over the salt police. Uncle Wang Congwu was arrested after that and was in jail in Daming until 1938, when the Guomindang let him and many other prisoners out to be stretcher bearers for the army when the Japanese came. The Communist Party soon sent him to Yanan [Communist Party headquarters], where he stayed throughout the war. I didn't know my uncle at that time.

The Japanese Come

I remember very well when the Japanese soldiers first came to Jiang Village. There were about three thousand of them. The people all tried to run away.

No one was prepared to stay and fight. I ran into the sand dune area two or three li from Jiang Village where there were trees and reeds to hide in. The women ran, too, to avoid being raped. People were very frightened and couldn't take care of each other. There was no organization to defend the village. The Japanese stayed for only one night. They lit fires in the streets and burned some houses, but no one was killed in Jiang Village.

When the Japanese troops got to Houhua Village there was a great massacre. There were two bandit gangs from north of here who often fought. They happened to be in Houhua, shooting at each other, when the Japanese approached the village. The Japanese thought they were being shot at and surrounded the village. Most people couldn't escape. The Japanese killed about three hundred people, about eighty of them from Houhua. All of them were men between eighteen and fifty years old. They didn't kill women, old people, or children. Many of the men who died were first stripped naked and forced into two houses which were then soaked with gasoline and set on fire. Everyone in them died.

The Japanese stayed only one day. After that a few more came with the "running dog" Imperial Assistance Army and other traitors to collect grain twice a year, after the summer and fall harvests. People buried as much grain as they could and ran away to hide in the sand area when the troops came. No one else from here was killed until April 12, 1941, when there was a big "mop-up" campaign.

The April 12, 1941, mop-up campaign was an attempt by the Japanese and their collaborators to get rid of Communist guerrillas. Thousands of Japanese troops using tanks and airplanes, accompanied by thousands more Chinese in the Imperial Assistance Army and other organizations that cooperated with the Japanese, attacked the Communist base in this area. Jiang Village was not attacked because it was controlled by the traitor Li Ying, nor was most of the area controlled by the religious-sect leader Sun Buyue, who was anti-Communist. No one in Jiang had joined the Communist-led guerrillas, but over seventy people in Houhua were in some sort of anti-Japanese armed force. Only six people from Houhua were killed, though, because most had run away. Many ran to the area controlled by the Imperial Assistance Army, especially to Bocheng market town, seven or eight li from Houhua, where they had relatives or friends who hid them. Houhua Village and Bocheng have a special relationship because years ago, Bocheng fought another village, and Houhua Village settled it. The people of Bocheng were grateful, and even today they are likely to help us.

About one hundred people were killed in Yuanhe Village, six li from here. A landlord from there who had met the Japanese in Zhao Village said they were not cruel, so people didn't run away. That is why so many people were killed there. Most of the Houhua people who died had run to the sand area around Qiankou Village, about eight li away. People from a lot of villages were hiding there in the reeds and trees and sand hills, but it turned out to be one of the centers of the Japanese attack. Hundreds of people were captured and put in stockades made from date trees that the Japanese and the traitors cut down by the tens of thousands. Then they were ma-chine-gunned and bayoneted. Over eight hundred people died in Qiankao, and thousands were killed elsewhere. Most of the houses in Qiankou were destroyed. It was part of the Japanese "burn all, kill all, loot all" policy.

Life was very hard in this area after the mop-up. The Japanese and trai-tors continued to come twice a year for grain, but gradually the Commu-nist-led guerrillas got stronger and stronger. Even Jiang Village eventually had to pay taxes to the guerrillas as well as to the traitor Li Ying. By 1945, Communist guerrillas were the principal force in Houhua and about thirty other villages nearby. This area was called an "old liberated area" by the Communist Party, but the guerrillas never had complete control. For in-stance, there was a village head in Houhua Village named Wang Xiantang who was in the Communist-led Eighth Route Army, but actually he was also a traitor and a spy for Japan. He was one of my uncles and lived oppo-site this house. He was found out when he sent his brother to Dongzhuang market town to give information to the Japanese collaborator Li Ying. His brother had no identification from Li Ying. People in Dongzhuang didn't know him or trust him. He was beaten and almost killed. When he re-turned to Houhua he quarreled with his brother. Activists and cadres heard the argument and began to learn the truth. They held meetings to criticize him. He could no longer be the village head. People often beat him, but they didn't kill him. Later he was driven out of the village and went to Shanxi Province as a beggar.

I did not join the guerrillas at that time. If I had been introduced to the guerrillas, I would have joined. At least then I would have had something to eat, but no one paid any attention to me. No one from Jiang Village joined the guerrillas, but there were four secret Communist Party members there. I didn't know they were Party members at the time, but I started to go to meetings at the house of someone named Peng. We discussed how the poor should get organized and how the land of poor people was grabbed by the rich households. If we owed them money and couldn't pay, we had to sell land to them bit by bit. They had all the wealth and gave us nothing. This kind of talk made a deep impression on me. They asked me to join the peasant association, and one evening, at a meeting in a grain mill, I did. There were no peasant association activities in Jiang Village because it was not advanced politically. When I returned to Houhua I would make more progress.

2

Return to Houhua Village: Land Reform and Establishing a Family, 1946–1953

In this chapter, Wang Fucheng recalls his return to Houhua Village, the evolution of his political activism, his marriage, and the growth of his family.

The land reform campaign that is the central focus of Wang Fucheng's narrative in this chapter was an essential part of the Communists' program to win the support of the impoverished peasantry in the several years before and after the establishment of a new government in China in 1949. Land reform proceeded in stages, beginning during the war years with a campaign to reduce rent on land and interest payments on borrowed money. After the war, the emphasis shifted to "settling accounts" with land owners who had not cooperated during the earlier campaign, and with those who had taken advantage of difficult times, such as the famine years, to purchase at bargain prices the land of desperate peasants. The next, more radical, step was classifying the rural populace into different social categories and coercively redistributing property from the relatively well-off to the relatively poor.

The process of confiscation and redistribution of property progressed at differing rates in different parts of China, depending on the degree of control the Communists had at a particular time and place. In north China, in the so-called "old liberated areas" where the Communists had established secure base areas during the war, the process of redistribution began as early as 1947. In most of south China, it had to be delayed until the early 1950s, when the Communists were in firm control. Houhua village was in an ostensibly old liberated area, but as Wang Fucheng's account clearly in-

dicates, Communist control there was tenuous, and political chaos was the norm in the late 1940s. Land redistribution could not be effectively implemented in Houhua until after the establishment of the People's Republic in late 1949.

The classification of the rural populace for the purpose of land redistribution was a complicated undertaking. It was no simple task to determine who belonged to what social class, particularly in a village where relative degrees of poverty, rather than a sharp division between rich and poor, was the main distinguishing characteristic. Delineation of social categories became increasingly complex as the process was implemented, but stated in their simplest form the categories were as follows: "landlord" households were those that owned land and rented it out, or hired others to cultivate it, doing no labor themselves; "rich peasant" households worked their own land, but also hired laborers or rented out surplus land; "middle peasant" households had enough land to sustain themselves without having to pay rent or work for others, but had no surplus land; "poor peasant" households were land owners, but their property was insufficient for subsistence, requiring them to work for others or rent land; and "hired laborers" owned no land and made a living only by working for others.

That the categorization process was somewhat arbitrary is evident in Wang Fucheng's account. There were no landlord households, properly defined, in Houhua Village, but two households had been classified as such simply because they were rich peasants who were considered particularly rapacious by their poorer neighbors. Recent research indicates that the Communists exaggerated the extent of landlordism in north China for political reasons, to mobilize the common people more effectively against the old rural elite. Readers should be aware that Wang Fucheng uses the term "landlord" in the loose, pejorative sense that had become common under the Communists.

Wang Fucheng discussed the early years of the Communist era in Houhua Village with enthusiasm and satisfaction. The process that transformed the social, economic, and political life of the village had dramatically improved his own life and brought him power, prestige, and enough to eat for the first time. Violence was an integral part of that process, and Wang Fucheng actively participated in it, first as part of a militia fighting to wipe out secret societies and later as a leader in the land reform campaign—a campaign designed to destroy the old rural elite as a class as well as to confiscate their property. Clearly he approved of the execution of the eighteen leaders of secret societies that he describes in this chapter, and he was unapologetic about the beatings that he administered during land reform. Having said that, it should be noted, in anticipation of chapters to come, that Houhua Village was unusually free of violence during Wang Fucheng's thirty-year tenure as Communist Party secretary. He based his

career on a belief in village unity and harmony, and he was largely success-
ful in realizing those traditional goals—even when the leadership of the
party that he represented actively promoted struggle and discord.

Wang Fucheng:
It is easy to say why I returned to Houhua Village. In 1946 both my
grandfather and grandmother died. My mother and I had acquired three
mud huts and two mu of land at the time. An uncle on my mother's side
wanted them. He came and put pressure on us to leave. He even stole our
cooking pot and bellows. We could no longer live there. The husband of
one of my aunts came from Houhua and took us back. We returned with
empty hands except for six logs that our Houhua relatives helped us buy
from Jiang.

My cousin Wang Zhuoru was away at the time. We lived in his small
kitchen house for almost a year. I was twenty-three, and my mother was
over fifty. We had one bed and one quilt between us. We borrowed a small
iron cooking pot and made a stove. I went out for firewood every day.
Sometimes I also cut weeds and dried them to sell for fuel. Some relatives
helped us with grain.

We got a house when a relative of ours, an old woman, died. Someone
asked me to take the part of a filial son at her funeral. I wore white mourning clothes and cried, acting in every way like her son. There was a daughter, but she was already married and living in another village. The family
then gave my mother and me eight mu of land and the shell of an aban-
doned house that had no roof because it had been burned by the Japanese.
Our relatives helped us build a roof with the logs we brought from Jiang
Village. We lived in that house until after liberation [1949]. We were able to
have a relatively peaceful life then, but we still didn't have enough to eat.

I remember that shortly after we returned to Houhua Village there was a
locust plague. That was in 1947 or 1948. One morning I saw the locusts in
the air. The sky was black with them, like a big cloud. You couldn't see the
sun, they were so thick. The large locusts with wings came first. I could
catch three or four at once in my hand. Then smaller insects came. The
plague lasted a long time, probably two months. Insects ate the crops completely—corn, sweet potatoes, even reeds. They ate everything. We dug
ditches to catch them, then we dried them for food. We have not had a locust plague since, though we have had a lot of locusts. When they get bad
now, the government sprays poison on them from airplanes.

After the war, when I returned, there was a campaign led by the Communist Party to reduce interest rates and the rent paid to landlords and to return confiscated land to peasant ownership. The situation was very complex. Many bandits and secret religious societies were still active. The
Communist Party was still a secret organization. Membership did not be-

come public until 1947, after the Guomindang had been defeated. Some people didn't dare take land. They feared that if Jiang Kaishek came back they would be punished.

Landlords and rich peasants were asked to decrease rent and interest rates and to raise the wages of laborers. Some of them thought it through and agreed to reduce rent and interest. Some even gave land as gifts to others. Others refused to give anything, still hoping for the return of the Guomindang.

In late 1946 the Guomindang did return. Its New Fifth Army came through chasing the [Communist] Eighth Route Army from south to north. The whole region fell under their control for about two months. The Eighth Route was not strong enough to hold them. A lot of irregular troops, bandits really, and a landlord army called the Homecoming Regiment came with the Guomindang. They killed a number of Communist Party members and cadres. No one was killed in Houhua, but thirteen new Communist Party members capitulated to the enemy and renounced their Communist affiliation. All of them had joined the Party in 1947. At that time anyone who wanted to join could, without even waiting for the usual one-year probation period. When those new members saw the New Fifth Army and the Homecoming Regiment return and witnessed battles every two or three days, they became frightened and left the Communist Party. Their political stand was not yet firm. None of the eight veteran Party members capitulated, and none was killed, though two were captured and thrown into the Nitrate River. They didn't drown. I didn't dare to speak at that time. I was not a cadre, but I was an activist in the land reform movement, so I kept quiet for two months until the bad people left. The Guomindang Fifth Army fled this area after the Eighth Route Army defeated them in a battle in Hebei Province north of here.

The bandits and irregulars withdrew too, but there were still a lot of bandits and secret religious society members in the area. In 1947 I joined the People's Militia to wipe them out. People had begun to know me by then, and I was accepted when I asked to join. Most of the time the militia worked in the fields, but we fought some battles. We fought mainly against the "local emperor" Sun Buyue[1] who controlled Hua and Xun counties. I remember chasing a branch of his organization out of Guoxiaozhai Village when we were stronger, and being chased out of Depizhuang when they were stronger. Eventually Sun Buyue escaped to Taiwan with Jiang Kaishek. The religious societies were not entirely wiped out until after liberation [1949–1950], when the new government controlled every county. Many of their members were put in jail. There was a jail here in Houhua where some were kept, because this was part of the old base area. Many of the worst landlords, rich peasants, and evil tyrants had joined the societies. They were investigated and tried, and the worst ones were killed. Eighteen of them were executed in the eastern part of this village, about two hundred meters from this house. The government had invited an opera troop to perform for three days before the execution to attract a lot of people. When everyone was assembled to watch the opera, the government announced the evil deeds of these counterrevolutionaries and bad elements. That is how the Communists educated people.

Land reform began again after the Guomindang New Fifth Army left. A work team of two or three people from the district came to promote it. Some were Communist Party members and some were not, but all represented the Party. They reorganized a peasant association and held meetings where people were told about the landlords' crimes and taught how to criticize them.

There were two rich peasant households in the village, those of Wang Yinchun and Wang Xuewu, and two landlord households, headed by Wang Demao and Wang Zengduo, who we called Wu Laoda. There were about 40 middle peasant households, 100 poor peasant households, and 10 hired laborers. The total land area was about 4,000 mu; 2,500 was crop land and 1,500 was salt land. The landlords and rich peasants owned almost two-thirds of the crop land, about 1,600 mu. Middle peasant families owned between 5 and 20 mu each, and poor peasants owned almost none—3.5 mu per family at most. Most earned their livelihood by making salt; 100 jin of salt was worth about 6 jin of grain. Some poor peasants and hired laborers worked long-term for rich peasants, and some worked only at harvest time; some begged. For a year's work, a full-time laborer would get about 500 jin of grain per year—200 would be wheat, the rest corn and sorghum. Part-time laborers worked by contract. They could get paid more if they worked more, and less if they worked less. In bad harvest years the amount was reduced. It took about 400–500 jin of grain per person to have enough to eat. Many ate less than that. People didn't eat much then, only porridge twice a day. In those days, each mu of crop land produced only 50–60 jin of winter wheat[2] and 70–80 jin of autumn crops (corn and sorghum). Today 500–700 jin of wheat is common. Eight hundred is the highest output.

During land reform I was not a Party member, but I was an activist working for the Party. I would do anything I was asked to do. I shouted slogans and went from house to house to collect people for meetings. I criticized the landlords, telling them to confess that their property came from us. I led people to their houses and brought their furniture to our office to be distributed to poor peasants. Sometimes we would go to the landlords' houses at night and beat them.

Wang Zengduo (Wu Loada) was the only person from this village who was killed during land reform. He had left the village and come back with the Guomindang. He wasn't really even a landlord. He had about 100 mu of land that he farmed himself as well as hiring others to help him, so he was really just a rich peasant. We called him a landlord because people hated him. So, you see, we had two criteria for landlord status—one was based on land and labor, and the other was based on the attitude of the masses. Wang Zengduo was the kind of person commonly referred to as *eba* (evil tyrant). If the poor went to his fields to scavenge after harvest, he beat them, especially women and children. Once he stripped naked a woman who was gleaning his field. This enraged the people. When the poor wanted to borrow anything, he would beat and curse them. His crimes were very serious. The poor peasants themselves decided he should be killed. We had an organization called the United Defense Brigade[3] that approved it. He was shot.

There were other sharp struggles in the village. We struggled against Wang Zengduo's widow in the east of the village. We hung her from a big tree with a rope tied to her hands behind her body. I was the director of the meeting. Most people taking part were women and children. They beat her to find out where she had hidden family property.

Wang Xuewu's wife is another example. Husbands often didn't know where property was buried; wives did. I took off my [cloth] shoe and beat her with it. She told me where property was buried. I took peasants to those places. Sometimes we found things, sometimes we didn't.

Wang Yingchun's wife was also hung from a tree and beaten. I shouted "Down with the landlords. If you don't confess, we'll hang you higher."

Redistribution of land was based on the number of people in each household. In this village each person was to get 1.5 mu of crop land. The amount differed according to the quality of the land. There were many arguments and much bitterness over the division of property. One rich peasant family didn't talk to their neighbors for several decades after land reform.

I got half an ox [shared with another family], five hundred bricks from rich people's houses that the poor peasants had destroyed, a wooden spade, and a manure fork. I didn't get any additional land because I already had eight mu from the relative who died. There were three in our household then. I had recently gotten married.

The marriage was arranged by my cousin Wang Zhuoru. One day he said to me, "You have been here for over two years. You have eight mu of land. I want to introduce you to a girl to marry." My cousin's wife said, "You are single, you should marry. There is a girl in our village whose family is very poor. It would be suitable to marry her." My wife's family lived in this village only seventy meters from here. Their name is Wang too, but it is a different Wang family.

My wife's uncle acted as go-between. My future wife and I didn't even know each other before we were married. That was feudalism. I went to her house with empty hands to talk to her mother. I went several times and each time talked to her mother, never to her. My wife at that time didn't like to talk. At first her mother said, my daughter is too young. She is only eighteen. You are seven years older.

Wang Xianghua, Wang Fucheng's wife, continues the story:

My mother listened to Wang Zhuoru's wife because they often worked together. They were both Communist Party members. In the struggle against the landlords in 1947, the poor were asked to register in the peasant association. Some dared to, some didn't. My mother dared to register and then to join the Party. As a Party member her duties were to go to meetings and struggle against the landlords. She mostly worked with women. My mother did what the Party told her to do. She told the women that they were equal to men and should leave their gates to go out and farm and help build socialist villages. Men were also educated by the Party and told not to bully women. A woman's organization was established, and the men became afraid to treat their wives badly. There were one or two cases where badly treated women got divorced. There were about thirty Party members in the village then, and ten of them were women. Today there are few women Party members, and none of those is active.

My mother never asked my opinion about the marriage. I had no opinion of my own. I didn't know Wang Fucheng. He had just come back from Jiang Village. My father and mother quarreled about the marriage. Father said, "Why should my daughter marry such a poor man?" But my father was dominated by my mother and couldn't decide anything in the family. My mother arranged everything; my father had nothing to do with it. I myself decided nothing.

There was no marriage ceremony at all. An old village woman came and asked me to go with her. I went to Wang Fucheng's house, where he and his mother lived in three rooms. We were too poor to ask any relatives to come. The first meal we ate was boiled cucumber. There was no meat at all. There was nothing to do about it if others laughed at us.

After the marriage I mostly stayed at home, weaving cotton cloth and selling it for more cotton. When necessary I did farm work in the fields, especially at harvest time when I cut crops. Our life gradually got better. We raised a donkey and a pig. Sometimes we even ate meat.

Wang Fucheng:

We never fought each other, but we have had arguments. It is funny. Once I got up in the dark and went to the threshing ground to see if there was a thief. I was a cadre then and very active in Party affairs. I thought that cadres should be models for others. I felt responsibility for the whole village, not just for my own family. My wife said sarcastically, "You are very active. If you get sick, who will take care of us?"

Sometimes we argued because I was trying to settle neighborhood disputes and she tried to persuade me not to look for trouble. I said, "It is my obligation to stop neighborhood quarrels." Our family quarrels have mostly been about my work as a cadre. For instance, I went to meetings all the time and came back late; I didn't have much time to grind wheat, which was a very difficult job. We had to pull millstones by ourselves or with animals. My wife was often in the mill house pulling the stone. Once I came home at about 10:00 P.M., and my wife complained bitterly to me, saying we shouldn't ask others to grind our wheat for us. She then asked me to do it, and although it was late and I was tired, I had no way out so I did it. I worked until midnight, when she came and told me to stop and continue in the morning. Later she said she was punishing me that way. When electricity came to the village in the late 1960s, one of the first things we did was buy an electric grinding mill.

When raising our son, Wang Dejun, we sometimes quarreled. My wife has a very hot temper. Mine is relatively calm. Sometimes she would say, "It is your turn to teach the child, but you say nothing. Are you dead?" It is difficult for me to get angry.

Wang Xianghua:
   Wang Dejun is our only child. He was born December 26, 1955. He went to school in this village when he was seven. All of the children did. He left school after junior secondary school when he was sixteen. He liked school and never ran away from it, but his grades were just average.

Wang Fucheng:
   When Wang Dejun graduated I was very busy working. We needed his labor and didn't want him to go to a higher-level school and then go out of the village to work. There were economic difficulties then, and we all decided he should stay home.

   Wang Dejun got married at age twenty in 1975. A relative acted as go-between. His wife's family lives in Lihetao, a village about eight li from here, near Jingdian. There were about ten in her household. They agreed to the marriage because I was a cadre and because my relatives were Wang Zhuoru and Wang Congwu. Their reputation was known around the villages. It was also because we didn't have any family problems.

   The couple first met in our village when she and her mother came to look at our situation. On the second visit they were engaged. We bought a set of clothes for the girl for several tens of yuan. Her family was also poor. At the time, it was not fashionable to buy furniture for a wedding.

Wang Xianghua:
   On the day of the wedding, Wang Dejun and two relatives went to his wife's village and brought her back with several other people. We did not

invite many people because large banquets were forbidden then. We are cadres and must set an example for other people. The marriage was registered with the local government. There was no special ceremony, but we had meat, eggs, and wine. They lived in the western courtyard of our compound in an old house made of brick. The house where they are now living is in the same location. It was built two years ago [1987]. Almost all of the villagers have built new homes in the past several years. Wang Dejun and his wife, Li Suzhen, have three children: a boy, Wang Yanwei, and two girls, Wang Yanxia and Wang Yongxia. In the past we couldn't imagine the happy life we have now.

3

"We Will Have a Bright Future": The Cooperative Movement and Joining the Communist Party, 1954–1957

After the land had been redistributed, the Communist Party launched a campaign in 1953 to collectivize the land and promote cooperative farming. The official rationale for collectivization was the supposition that land and labor could be used more efficiently—and the product of labor could be distributed more equitably—if the land were not privately owned. Also, the Party looked forward to the day when farming would be mechanized, and it reasoned that the existing small, irregular plots of land would be ill-suited to that technological advance.

Collectivization proceeded in stages. The first, or lower, stage was referred to as "semisocialist"—farming was cooperative, but land, tools, and animals (except those purchased jointly by the cooperative) were still privately owned. The harvest was divided on the basis of both the property and the labor contributions of each household. The second stage cooperatives were called "fully socialist." Productive property (not houses) was now collectively owned, and distribution was calculated solely on the basis of the labor contribution of each individual. It was assumed that in the second stage, efforts to enhance equity and efficiency begun in the first stage would be advanced. Whereas the first stage was voluntary, the second was mandatory.

It is clear from Wang Fucheng's account that collectivization was never popular in Houhua Village. In the first, voluntary stage, only 13 percent of the households joined cooperatives. Most of them were the poorest house-holds, those that had the least to lose or the most to gain by pooling their resources; and even some of those households tried to drop out in the first year. The Party had a lot at stake in the campaign and tried to assure its success by cutting off credit to all households except those in the coopera-tives. With exclusive access to low-interest loans, members of the new co-operatives indeed did better by farming together than they had previously done separately—and better than some of the households that had refused to join—but most of the villagers were not sufficiently impressed to rush into the fully socialist cooperatives when the government began to promote them a year later.

Wang Fucheng's account of the process by which people were induced to join second stage cooperatives is an excellent example of the methods pre-ferred by the Communist Party to assert its will: Patient and persistant ver-bal pressure, and ultimately criticism and threats, wore down resistance and achieved results. Violence supplemented gentler methods of persuasion in many villages, but it was never employed in Houhua Village during the cooperative movement or at any other time after the early stages of the land reform campaign.

Wang Fucheng had been a vigorous advocate of collectivization, and as we shall see in a later chapter, he was loathe to give it up in the early 1980s, when the Party decided to decollectivize; but his perceptive and succinct as-sessment of the strengths, and especially the weaknesses, of cooperative farming is comprehensive and dispassionate.

He is less clear-sighted on the issue of women. Wang Fucheng was not overtly a male chauvinist, but like most rural males with whom I have spo-ken, Wang felt that assigning fewer work points, and thus less pay, to fe-males as a group was justified by the generally greater physical strength of males. The fact that even the strongest female received fewer work points than the weakest male for doing the same job did not seem to matter, nor did the fact, as Wang said in a later statement, that women did most of the farm work during the period of collectivization. As a loyal Communist, Wang Fucheng subscribed to Mao Zedong's slogan that "Women hold up half the sky," but as a rural male, he felt that they should not be paid as much for doing it.

Wang Fucheng:

In 1953 another work team from the government came to our village to mobilize us for a different stage of development. Most members of the work team were from the township. They were rural people, peasants, though some were office workers from Neihuang. The only one I remember who came from a large city was a man named Ge, a bureau head who came to inspect the work.

The work team held village meetings and told us that if we joined the land association and formed cooperatives we would have a bright future. We would plow without oxen [i.e., with tractors], light our houses without oil [electricity], and have machines for all work. I was an activist promoting this movement, but many people didn't wish to join. Some said we would have no freedom if we joined the association. One said, "We are all so poor. How can we have a happy future just by joining an association?" He and others didn't believe all of the things the cadres were telling us.

There were about 300 households in the village then. About forty joined the land association and formed two cooperatives. Almost all who joined were poor. They had gotten land in the land reform, but it was not enough. Some had already sold some land. Only those with the least land joined the association. No one was forced to join. The cadres said to let them wait; sooner or later all would join, all would follow the socialist road. The cooperatives were first-level cooperatives: We pooled our animals and farmed the land together, but we still owned our land and tools. What we received at harvest time was based on both the amount of our property and the amount of work we did. This would change in the higher-level cooperatives, when all land would be owned collectively and distribution would be based on labor alone. These low-level cooperatives lasted two years.

The township government supported us by giving us advice and lending us money at low rates of interest. We borrowed from a credit association of the township government. No money was lent to individual farmers outside the cooperative. We bought donkeys, horses, mules, and two horse carts.

In the early stage of the cooperative, some people wanted to drop out. The cadres talked to them, and most were persuaded to stay in. Most of us who joined listened to Chairman Mao's call and were fully dedicated in heart and mind. Men and women worked together in the field. We didn't quarrel. After the first harvest we got more than those who worked alone because they couldn't manage as well and also because the government gave us some help. We paid back the loan after the harvest. The fence sitters became firm in the cooperative, but it was impossible to attract new members to the two lower-level cooperatives because the membership was already settled and there would have been accounting problems. No new lower-level cooperatives were formed in the village.

I was the manager of the land association. I was illiterate, but the villagers asked me to serve. I also became leader of the cooperative and then village leader at that time. There are two main leaders in the village. The top leader is the Party branch secretary, who is in charge of all village affairs and of Party work in the village. The village leader is second in importance. He is in charge of all farm work. I was not yet a Party member, though I had applied and been recommended many times. I wanted to make rapid progress, but the wife of my cousin Wang Zhuoru prevented me from joining. She was Wang Zhuoru's first wife. She was also an early Communist Party member and a cadre. Wang Zhuoru had another wife outside the village, and the Party didn't allow cadres to have two wives, so they told him to divorce this first wife. She was very angry and took revenge on our family. Some of our relatives went outside the village to join the Party.

I became village leader in 1954. The former village leader feared the difficulties that were occurring in the village and didn't want to be leader any longer. Many people were like him. There were many problems, and the villagers were scared. I feared nothing. Before the cooperative movement, the village leader was not selected in a village meeting, as I was. He was selected by people of high reputation in the village, not cadres but village elders. After liberation he was selected by leaders in the poor peasants association. They then asked the villagers, and if there was no disagreement, it was settled. Most village leaders served only one or two years. Village affairs were difficult, and leaders were paid only several dou of grain extra. Most people felt that it was too little for all the problems. It was not easy to be a village leader—you needed a good temper, you couldn't get mad, but most people did.

When I became leader, the branch Party members were looking for someone capable and advanced politically. I was not backward, and all the village people said I was upright. To tell you the truth, all of the people knew of my activism, and everyone trusted and supported me. The cadres from outside knew and trusted me, too. They saw with their own eyes that I was upright. I was reasonable and could settle disputes between people. I would go on my own where there were fights. I feared nothing. I had done no bad deeds and had a high reputation. Also, I was a model in farm work. I was very short and not so strong, but strong enough to carry a load of 120 jin [about 122 lbs.]. My farm-work ability was just so-so compared to others, but I tried very hard all the time. I was selected village leader at a large meeting attended by township and county cadres. All the village people said I was capable, so I was appointed, and the county government approved.

Higher-Level Cooperatives

In 1956 an outside work team came again to mobilize us for higher-stage cooperatives. All the land would now be pooled; there would be no more private ownership. There was much disagreement, but people had no choice. Some had more land and animals than others. Do you think they were willing to join the cooperatives? But for the poor there was no other way, so we held meetings every day to persuade people to join. We could not have persuaded those with more property to join if we had not had those meetings. They were held on a threshing ground east of the village. We also held small meetings and talked to people individually in their homes. We watched the numbers of those who registered. The first day 100 households, then 120, 140, and so on. This went on for several months. We kept talking about the bright future. Cadres from the township and county came and read materials from the central government. They promised machines to till the land, electricity, telephones, and more wells. I did this, too. I couldn't read or write, but I worked with my mouth. Persuasion was very difficult. Many people argued with us and even cursed us, but we paid no heed if they didn't do bad deeds. Some hid their farm tools. Some lay on the ground and refused to work. Actually, even many of those who joined the cooperative were not enthusiastic. They signed the register, but in their hearts they didn't join.

Finally, we severely criticized backward people, even mentioning their names to shame them. There was a villager named Wang Wuniu who picked a fight with a county cadre named Liu Fengxian who often came here. Wuniu attacked him with his belt and an axe. I criticized him severely at a large meeting of all the association members. After the meeting I went to his house. I said, "Is this situation your fault? If you don't work hard to produce grain, how can our country get enough support from us?" Eventually he admitted it was his fault, and we settled the question. Another old man nicknamed Ergouwen went looking for Liu Fengxian. His belt was in his hand. He was shouting and crying. He said he was short of grain. People were afraid he would hurt himself. I tried to calm him, and then I criticized him. I said, "You are old enough, where is your face? Don't you still want face?[1] You talk so much nonsense." After that he calmed down. Public opinion at that time was divided, but there were more quarrels than fights. No one was arrested.

Eventually we used a new method. Two long tables were set up—one on the west side for those who had joined, and one on the east side for those who hadn't. A representative from each of the thirty or forty households that hadn't joined stood behind the east table facing the majority behind the west table. Gradually, after much discussion and persuasion, those on the east side started coming to the west side. Their numbers decreased to twenty, to ten, to five. Finally, everyone joined. The whole village formed one large cooperative.

I was still not in the Party, but I was doing the Party secretary's work in this campaign. I was called an instructor. I was also elected to be the leader of the cooperative. The cooperative members elected me themselves. There were no cadres from outside at the meeting. Finally, I joined the Party. A cadre named Wang Degao from this village introduced me. All the Party members said I should have been admitted long ago. The people all said,

"We can't settle problems without Wang Fucheng. Let him join the Party."
The one-year probation requirement for joining the Party was waived, and
I was immediately made vice branch secretary. Soon I became Party secretary, the highest leadership position in the village. I held that position for
the next thirty years.

In the first year of the higher-stage cooperatives, 1956, there were a lot of
locusts. It could have been a disaster, but the government killed them with
poison dropped from airplanes. The weather was good that year, and we
had a good harvest of wheat, corn, and sorghum. The harvest was better
than before, but only because of the weather. In fact, in the first three years
of the advanced cooperatives we increased production, but beginning in
1957 we wasted a lot. There were many problems and much dissatisfaction. Even the cadres were divided about the value of cooperatives.

My uncle Wang Congwu came back to the village for a visit in 1957 and
stayed in my house one night. Most people in the village called him grandfather or uncle. He was then the North China Military District political
commissioner. One day the Party secretary of the county and county police
came with him to see me. I still remember what we discussed. My uncle
said, "We have now reached the second stage in cooperativization. The
peasants now all work together. Are they satisfied?" I said, "Some yes,
some no. Those with complaints mostly have problems with grain. Some
have grain stored but deny it. Others really are short."

Almost the whole village had gathered here to see Wang Congwu. They
talked, they shouted, some even cried. Someone said, "You are a high-level
cadre, can't you bring grain? Please make a speech." My uncle told the
county Party secretary to make a speech. It was a cold day, but the secretary
was frightened and was sweating a lot. He kept wiping his brow because a
high-level cadre was beside him when he was making a speech about policy.
He said, "Don't worry about a lack of grain, we will discuss it later. I have
none here now."

I then said to the excited crowd, "Let the secretary and uncle leave." But
an old woman of about seventy who kept weeping tried to stop them from
leaving. Wang Congwu then told me to solve that particular problem. I decided to give her fifty jin of grain the next day. In this way they managed to
leave.

The collective system lasted here from 1956 through 1984. Today the
land is still collectively owned, but it is not collectively farmed. Each household now has an allotment of land for which it is responsible. There were
some good things about the collective system, and some bad. It will never
be reestablished because production is much higher now and the people
don't want to go back.

The advantage of the collective system was that we did a lot of things together that the individual households could not do for themselves. For in-

stance, we filled in and leveled the land to the east of the village where the Nitrate River Gulch had been. There is now crop land where none had been before. We also dug irrigation trenches and wells together. I was very much in favor of the collective system and worked hard to fulfill the Party's plan, but I now see that there were more problems than benefits.

The main problem was that the masses didn't have any freedom; they just had to follow the cadres' orders. They had no choice about when to work and when to stay home. If they didn't work, they would be criticized and people would continually shout slogans at them. So, often, people went to work, but they did little. We had a big bell in the village that we rang when it was work time. After a while when we rang it the first time in the morning, no one came. Then cadres had to go to people's houses and ask them to go to the fields. At 8:00 or 9:00 A.M. people were still in their houses. Then they would go to work, but they chatted and rested a lot. When the production team leaders urged them to work faster, they wouldn't because they said, "When we work hard we don't see much grain for all our effort. Where is the result?"

Part of the problem was that the government took most of the grain. It allotted 360 jin per person to keep and bought the rest, but it did not pay a very high price—only about half of what is paid today. There was also a grain tax—that is, grain that we gave to the government for no payment. It was based on both land amount and output at harvest time. When output was good, we paid more tax, so there was little incentive. The truth is that people often couldn't produce enough for their own consumption. There was a popular expression, *"Gou bu gou sanbailiou"* (360 jin was all we got whether it was sufficient or not).

The grain was not distributed equally, it was done according to work points. We calculated the amount of grain that remained for eating after government tax and purchase and evaluated how much grain to give for each work point. Those with more work points got more grain. The full allotment of work points for a day's work was ten points for men and seven points for women. Women got fewer points because they are weaker and can't do some jobs as well as men, such as plowing the fields, breaking up the soil with hoes, and digging manure from pits. That was the real reason for work-point difference between males and females. It wasn't because of feudal attitudes.

Work-point distribution was determined by the production team leaders and by representatives elected by the masses. They chose people who were impartial. Some were representatives for years. In cases where there were disputes and quarrels, meetings were held that included brigade leaders, team leaders, the representatives, and those who had complaints. Sometimes the masses were included, too. Most of the complaints were by lazy people.

One thing that made grain distribution unequal, resulting in bad feelings, was that some of the production teams had higher output than others. For instance, team number six often produced about twice as much as team number three. Distribution for team members was based on production by their particular team and not by the whole village or brigade. The problem was not with the amount or quality of land. That was about the same for all teams. It was mainly due to a difference in leadership and management, and how well the masses worked. There were quarrels and fighting in the less productive teams. The leaders and masses blamed each other. I often went to work with teams with lower output and tried to find the causes. The problem was usually the leadership. Generally we didn't remove cadres from their positions. I did that only once. That was because the leader lied about the team's cotton output, giving a much lower figure than was actually the case. Several months later I asked that person to be leader again. Usually I would go to leaders' houses to educate them if they had taken advantage of their positions. For instance, I would say, "Why should you take materials owned by the collective for yourself? You are too selfish. What kind of example is that for the masses?"

Actually, many leaders didn't want to be cadres. There were 300–400 people in a team, each with his own heart and mind. It was difficult to be a cadre. Organization and management work was difficult, and the pay was not much better than that of the ordinary worker. Team leaders were assigned a full ten work points per day whether they were in the fields or in meetings. They got extra points for evening meetings, and usually at the end of each year they got 20–30 full days' extra work points as compensation. The amount depended on how well the team had done that year. But even with the extra pay, many people didn't think it was worth it.

There was another important reason why production was lower under the collective system. There were too many leaders and too many meetings. For almost thirty years there was an average of eight meetings every ten days. Those meetings involved almost half the able-bodied male laborers. Each of the six teams had seven cadres—the team leader, two vice team leaders, an accountant, a trustee for public property, a militia leader, and a women's team leader. The brigade [village] had twelve leaders in addition to the separate team leaders. Most of these leaders were able-bodied men. Because they spent most of their time in meetings and not in production, the women did most of the farm work.

Today there are almost no meetings, and people work much harder on their own allotment of land than they worked for the collective. Production has increased greatly since decollectivization began here in 1983. There is no question, however, that if the land were still collectivized, production would have increased anyway, maybe even as much as today. There is no way to compare. What we lacked in those days was electricity, water, and fertilizer. We might be just as well off, and the people would have had more security than they have today. Still, people do not want to go back to the collective system. The difference today is that they have more freedom. They don't have to go to the fields every day. Things are more under their control. They can spend on marriages and funerals if they want to. They want that freedom. That is the farmer's mentality.

4

"This Is Not the Way to Do Farm Work": The Great Leap Forward, 1958–1960

The period in which the farmers of Houhua Village had the least freedom, the least control over their lives, was at the end of the 1950s during a campaign known as the "Great Leap Forward." The name is ironic, for ultimately the campaign proved to be a great leap backward. It began in 1958 with the confident prediction that China would leap beyond Great Britain in industrial production in fifteen years (a feat requiring an eightfold increase in output) and leap beyond the Soviet Union in the transition from socialism to communism at the same time. It ended three years later with a 14 percent decline in industrial production and an agricultural disaster in the countryside that demographers estimate cost thirty million lives throughout China.

The way to accomplish a great leap, according to Communist Party Chairman Mao Zedong, was to "put politics in command"; that is, to rely on human will and other such subjective factors to overcome all material obstacles. Mao felt that China had been underutilizing its resources, especially its human resources. He sought to mobilize those resources by "walking on two legs"—by using methods that were both modern and traditional, capital-intensive and labor-intensive, foreign and domestic. During the first five-year plan (1953–1957), the growth of agricultural output had lagged far behind that of industrial output, in part because capital investment had been allocated primarily to the urban sector of the economy. The "walking on two legs" approach would try to balance a largely capital-intensive industrial policy with a mainly labor-intensive agricultural policy.

That could be achieved most effectively and economically, it was felt, by enlarging collective enterprise in the countryside and introducing a greater degree of regimentation to the lives of the people. Thus, in August 1958, it was decided to merge a number of agricultural cooperatives to form "communes." By the end of that October the process was basically completed throughout the country. Communes were designated the lowest level of state government. They were to be largely self-sufficient units that combined farming, manufacturing, commercial, educational, and military functions. They would be large enough to mobilize labor and capital for fairly large-scale projects (such as leveling the land or establishing a small factory) and small enough to encourage local initiative and innovation.

Administratively, they functioned on three levels—the commune, the brigade, and the team. Typically, commune headquarters were located in the former subcounty administrative units known as townships. Villages within a township were designated "brigades," and each brigade was divided into several teams. Houhua Village was one of twenty-two brigades that constituted Liucun Township Commune. The population of the commune was about 25,000 people. The 1,400 people of Houhua Brigade were divided into six teams of approximately 233 people each.

Wang Fucheng's discussion of the Great Leap Forward policies as they were applied in Houhua Village makes readily apparent why the effort failed so disasterously throughout the country. He spoke with weary disdain of the blunders of nonfarming cadres who had been sent to villages to guide agricultural work. His wife, Wang Xianghua, was more openly derisive in ridiculing the hypocrisy and dishonesty engendered by Great Leap imperatives.

This chapter is particularly revealing of Wang Fucheng's character and leadership ability. Confronted by potentially disasterous directives from above, he was able to protect the interest of the village while remaining basically loyal to the Party. He is typically modest in describing his own role during the Great Leap Forward, but it is to his lasting credit that no one in Houhua Village starved to death in the great famine that reduced the population of all of the surrounding villages at that time.

Wang Fucheng:

In mid-1958 cadres from the county and township came to the village and took over all farming decisions. This was the beginning of the Great Leap Forward. We worked three shifts a day. We got up at 5 A.M. and worked until breakfast at 8 A.M., then we worked until supper in the evening, and after that we worked at night. We were urged to do two days' work in one day. In the beginning we all supported the cadres and constantly shouted slogans. At times I was so busy I didn't have time to eat. We were afraid of wasting time, so we moved our cooking stoves and pots to the field. Thirty or forty people shared the same pot. Sometimes we slept in the fields at night. We were organized into a military system. The village was a battalion with companies, platoons, and squads under it. I was the battalion political instructor in charge of all Party matters. The village leader was the battalion commander in charge of farming affairs. We used loudspeakers to criticize those who made mistakes and to praise those with merit. I remember a man named Wang Dehui who slept in the field instead of working after we moved our cooking materials there. I severely criticized him at a meeting, saying, "Your thought is not correct. If all are like you, how can we have a happy life?" Wang Dehui had criticized the Great Leap Forward as unreasonable.

Wang Dehong also criticized it, saying, "You support socialism and shout a lot, but I don't see that you raise more crops." His family had been richer than others. I put a high hat [a dunce cap] on him and said: "You are unsatisfied with socialism. If people believe you, how will the poor be able to lead a happy life? They work day and night and think the Great Leap Forward is a good movement."

Village leaders had no right at that time to decide what to plant and what not to plant. The county and township government planned everything. They said to plant corn, sorghum, and especially sweet potatoes. We planted 1,000 mu of sweet potatoes that year, and they grew very well. About twenty-two villages in this area ate sweet potatoes from our fields. But we didn't even have time to harvest them all because the outside cadres were in such a rush to plant the next crop. They paid little attention to the harvest but mainly concentrated on planting winter wheat. Then they reported to the township and county government how fast they had done their job. If they planted wheat fast, the government would praise them. Otherwise they were criticized. A nearby village, Weihuang, had been told to plant peanuts. At harvest, in their rush to plant the next crop, they just pulled up the stems and leaves and left most of the peanuts in the ground. Then they plowed the land and planted other crops so the cadres could report that their work had been done very fast. Some of our sweet potatoes rotted in the ground for the same reason. What we did dig up, we dried in pieces. To keep them during the winter we buried them in the ground, but they rotted after two months. We distributed them to the villagers, but they didn't want rotten potatoes. They were hungry and dissatisfied.

When we planted the winter wheat we were told to dig deep, one or two chi [1 chi = N meter]. An animal pulling a plow couldn't dig that deep, so we had to do it with spades. A cadre from outside the village said, "An ox can't dig as much as a human." We all listened to this cadre's words, but we knew that they were nonsense. We were also told to sow forty to fifty jin of wheat seed per mu instead of the usual eighteen jin. In Dongjiang Village next to us they were told to use 120 jin. We had to spread the seed with our spades because the planting box couldn't sow it in that quantity.

I still didn't have any doubts about the Party's general policy, but I knew in my heart that that was not the way to plant crops. Is it right to waste so much seed? Is it right to cut crops at night? I did not argue with the township and county cadres, but sometimes I said what was true: "That is not the way to do farm work."

We worked in the fields day and night, but often we were forced to waste time. For instance, when visiting groups came from different places, sometimes two or three times a day, we had to greet them, shouting slogans and saying, "Welcome! Welcome!" Sometimes when we were working in the east field, we had to go welcome them in the west. Sometimes when we were working in the west, we had to go welcome them in the east. I was the leader of the village, and I showed my dissatisfaction to the outside cadres. They criticized me for rightist tendencies and said I was lagging behind the developing situation. I dared not reply, but I thought, "I have been a farmer for half of my life, and you have just come from the county town. You cannot know farming better than I. You are directing blindly." All of the village cadres and masses were dissatisfied, but they had to follow the outside cadres' orders. This situation lasted for over a year. The movement eventually failed because the masses were dissatisfied.

At harvest time we were under a lot of pressure to exaggerate the amount of grain production. Many cadres made mistakes on this issue. Many villages gave a "Great Leap Forward report" when they reported their harvest. If they harvested 400 jin of grain, they would say 500 or 700 jin. The higher the report, the more praise from the commune cadres. If the report was low, they were criticized. We had meetings almost every day to report output. I was honest—I didn't exaggerate—so I was severely criticized. A cadre said to me, "Why is production in your village so low compared to others? You are the leader. There is a problem with your thought. If the villages don't give grain, how can the country run? We must think first of the nation, then of the village." I replied that I was reporting true figures; I didn't exaggerate.

Did I ever lie? Did I ever report false figures? Yes. I had to tell lies. We all did. When cadres from outside the village held a meeting to struggle against a village cadre, I had to protect him. They wanted us to estimate the production amount for the next harvest. When that harvest came, we reported the real figure. They kept asking us to give a higher figure until they were satisfied. They asked, "Why is the output in your village so low? Is it because you are lazy or the masses are lazy? Why is the situation in other villages so much better than in yours? Where is your grain? Did you hide it? Did the wind blow it away? Did it rot on the threshing ground?" They told us to find the cause for such low production. Under this pressure we all told lies. Actually, the villages were beginning to run short of grain.

After we had reported the grain amount to the outside cadres, each village had to decide how much grain to give to the government. I'll give you an example that is an approximation, not the real figures. If we had a grain output of 30,000 jin, we might keep 20,000 to eat, save 5,000 for various uses in the brigade, and give 5,000 to the government. The government didn't pay us for that amount. We called it "patriotic grain." Villages that reported very high grain production figures had to give a greater amount to the government. Because of false production reports, there was not enough to eat. The masses' enthusiasm fell. Outside cadres said we had enough to eat, but that wasn't true. They said we had a lot of grain in storage, but actually we had almost nothing.

It wasn't the weather that caused this shortage, as some officials said later. It was humans who made the disaster. I remember that there was a flood that affected this village at that time, but it wasn't too serious. Only some fields were flooded. Bad management was the cause of the disaster.

The Great Leap was supposed to be a leap in making steel and digging ditches as well as in agriculture. In late 1958 my wife went to Anyang City to work for a steel plant during a national campaign to make iron and steel. Thirty-four men and sixteen women from our village went to Anyang.

Wang Xianghua continues the story:

I was in Anyang from the eighth month [of the lunar calendar] until three months later. I lived there in a tent. I drank only from muddy ponds and ate corn porridge. We all ate together without food coupons. My job was to break up stones and load them into a furnace. My husband was a cadre, and being his wife, I had to work actively.

Wang Fucheng:

I had a lot of difficulties at that time. I was working too hard and coughed up a lot of blood. We had a two-year-old son. When my wife went to Anyang, we had to send him to live with his maternal grandmother who lives about 100 meters from here. Grandmother was also a Party member and had to go to meetings. She once locked the house and left the child sleeping on the bed. She was gone three hours, and when she came back she couldn't find him. She finally found him naked in a basket that had some cotton in it. He had cried for a long time. There were a lot of tears on his face. She was very upset and cried, too. Another time she went to a meeting and left the door open. The baby fell from the bed and crawled out the door to the outside gate of the courtyard. He couldn't get out, but he sat there and cried. An outside cadre heard him and called a neighbor, who picked him up and tried to dress him.

I was very displeased and in low spirits when this happened. There were two provincial-level cadres here at the time. One asked why I was so dejected. I told him the truth, and he immediately sent a letter ordering that my wife be sent back to take care of the baby. The next day a cadre went to Anyang to bring her back. The provincial cadre also asked about my attitude toward village work. I said no matter how hard the work, I would put the affairs of the village first.

In late 1958 we established a commune in this area. Liucun Township (which had political jurisdiction over twenty-two natural villages) became the commune headquarters. The twenty-two villages each became production brigades. We had six production teams under the brigade in this village. I was the top leader in the brigade.

We built a large building in the field as a big eating hall and also for holding meetings and sleeping. Actually, it was a very simple structure made of corn and sorghum stalks. We also had a "happiness home," sometimes called a courtyard, for nurturing the old; a children's courtyard; and a maternity courtyard. The "happiness home" was right here in this courtyard, which belonged to Wang Zhuoru at the time. There were three rooms where about twenty old people lived. I once sent three young people there as well to recuperate from the swelling disease (edema) caused by hunger.

Wang Xianghua:

I was the head of the children's courtyard. I also worked in the maternity courtyard. We gave women twenty jin of white flour and three jin of sugar if they came there to have their babies. If they didn't come, they got nothing. We did away with all of those things when the Great Leap Forward ended. The people didn't like them. Actually, for the most part, they were all just forms. At that time, the form was more important than the reality. People talked a lot and shouted a lot of slogans, but they didn't do so much work.

Wang Fucheng:

We had to talk and shout a lot because there were so many struggles against those who didn't. The cadres judged people by their attitudes. If they talked and shouted, the cadres would say their attitude was good.

When the commune was set up, we also trained a militia. This is an old base area with a long tradition of citizen soldiers. They existed long before liberation and even before the War of Resistance. In those earlier times only some of the villagers were in the militia, but during the Great Leap Forward, almost all labor hands joined. We still have a militia today, but there is no training. After the Cultural Revolution, the weapons of the militia were taken away by the county government. We don't allow people to own guns.

After the first year of the Great Leap Forward, outside cadres no longer had control of farming. The brigade and team leaders could decide what to plant and where to plant it. Also at that time, the work-point system was restored and we added extra workpoints for extra work. When the Great Leap Forward began, we did not count work points, we just counted family members and distributed the harvest on the basis of need, not on the basis of work.[1]

After we were in charge of farming decisions again, I asked the people here to plant a lot of turnips because turnips were not taxed. That is one of the main reasons that people here did not starve during the Great Leap Forward famine. The government only wanted wheat after the summer harvest and corn and dried sweet potatoes in the fall. They didn't want our turnips, so we got by on those. I still didn't exaggerate grain output. If I had, most people in my village would have had the swelling disease, and some would have died from hunger because we would have had to give more grain to the government. I could do things that other people dared not do because of my uncle's influence. The situation in this village was better than other villages, so many people wanted to marry their daughters into this village.

The Great Leap Forward lasted for over two years. It stopped in 1960. No one in this village died of hunger or cold at that time, but a lot of people from other villages did. Three died in Zhonghua Village next to us, and in Caopo Village Bocheng Commune, several li from here, an average of one person a day died of hunger for a period of time. We must analyze concretely why they died. Generally it was because the local cadres did not pay enough attention to people's problems. I took care of the health of the villagers. I knew of three people who almost died of starvation. Their legs began to swell, and medicine had no effect. I knew the swelling was because of hunger. One was a young man of twenty-five. The other two were old people. I sent them all to the courtyard for nurturing the old and let them rest there for a month. I gave them 1.5 jin of grain per day rather than the usual one jin. They gradually recovered.

There were lots of digging projects at the time. People from here went to widen the Nitrate River and to dig an irrigation canal from the Wei River to Puyang County. You can still see it. They were not paid for that work. It was all volunteer. The village had to support them.

Some of our people went to Neihuang town to help dig a 1,000-mu fish pond in the winter. The three people from Zhonghua Village who died of cold and hunger died there. They were asked to work day and night but were not given anything to eat. I took great care of the people from here who went to dig the fish pond. I went there to check them and asked our people to send them two carts of turnips, dried sweet potato slices, and some grain. I persuaded those still in the village to eat less and support those digging the pond. Our villagers survived. When they returned I immediately sent them to the courtyard for nurturing the old and let them rest.

A government inspection team came to this village three times to see why our production figures were so low. A secretary of my uncle Wang Congwu came twice. Wang Congwu was then Secretary of the Central Government Inspection Bureau. His secretary lived in the commune headquarters for one or two days and spent one night in my house. The ordinary masses didn't know he was my uncle's secretary. He checked the production figures in our village account book. I was not struggled against because my uncle was Wang Congwu. It was not because he protected me purposely, but everyone knew of his influence and our relationship, so I was only asked to pay attention to my words.

After the secretary reported the real situation in this and other villages to the central government, they realized that the living standard was poor in the countryside. Beijing ordered Henan Province to stop what it had been doing. Finally the central government sent aid—wheat, sweet potatoes, sugar, and fish. The people were joyful. Other villages also got aid, as did other counties, for instance, Hua and Xun counties nearby. There had been a lot of suffering in this area during the Great Leap Forward, and we had a great feeling of relief when it was finally over.

5

"Five Winds," "Three Togethers," "Four Cleanups," and Other Campaigns, 1961–1965

The years following the Great Leap Forward were characterized by a struggle within the Communist Party to determine the path that socialism would take in China. That struggle culminated in 1966 with the initiation of the "Great Proletarian Cultural Revolution." The issues in the struggle were complex, but two were particularly salient—collectivity and class struggle. In the face of criticism during and following the great famine, Mao Zedong sought to preserve the communes and the concept of collective production–collective reward. He also advocated continuing class struggle based on his contention that people in official positions would abuse their power and become exploiters unless they were continually monitored by the masses. Those who disagreed with him he characterized as class enemies who were "taking the bourgeois road."

Though no one dared to oppose Mao openly after his uncompromising attack on an early Great Leap critic, General Peng Dehuai, in mid-1959, there were many Party members who worked behind the scenes to modify Mao's policies. They favored less collectivity and more individual incentives, and they had a greater tolerance for disparity of wealth if it served to promote production. Furthermore, they emphasized social harmony rather than class struggle, and orderly, incremental change initiated from above rather than locally implemented mass criticism of cadres and chaotic "great leaps forward."

It is apparent from Wang Fucheng's account of those years that he was not aware of the struggle taking place in the higher ranks of the Party. In discussing the "Five Winds" and "Socialist Education" campaigns in this

*chapter, he does not mention policy changes that represented opposing fac-
tional initiatives during the campaigns. There were, in fact, two phases of
the Five Winds campaign. The first began in late 1959 and condemned certain manifestations of Great Leap policies; the second began two years
later and was critical of the effects of measures adopted in the first phase.
"Wind" in colloquial Chinese connotes tendencies or practices. The five
practices condemned in the early campaign were ultracommunism (such as
collectivizing cooking utensils and other household items, and overempha-
sizing the free supply of necessities such as food in order to realize the
Communist slogan "to each according to need"; such practices were said to
be ultra-egalitarian and to preclude incentives to work hard); exaggeration
(in reporting production figures); commandism (coercion); special privi-
leges for cadres; and blind leadership of production (giving orders when
you do not know what you are doing).*

*This first phase of the campaign, which was directed at local cadres, was,
in part, a transparent attempt to shift the blame for Great Leap failures
from upper-level policy makers to lower-level policy implementers; but
when juxtaposed with the second phase, or the "New Five Winds" campaign, the first phase can be read as a criticism of Great Leap policies in
general, and thus of Mao Zedong himself. The New Five Winds were Mao's
response. They were critical of measures that had been adopted to counter-
act what Mao's detractors regarded as the excesses of the Great Leap.
Those measures included a degree of decentralization (the team became the
basic unit of accounting, replacing the commune); the return of small private plots to peasants; reauthorization of household side-line production;
reintroduction of limited free markets; and a general relaxation of surveil-
lance of local cadres. Mao asserted that such measures had been responsible for a general breakdown in discipline and a consequent reemergence of
corrupt practices. He identified the New Five Winds as: taking independent
action; speculating and profiteering; stealing; gambling; and feudal superstition (the return of traditional religious practices). To correct these winds,
Mao directed the party to launch the "Socialist Education Campaign in the
Countryside."*

*The dispute within the Party over the Socialist Education Campaign was
not about whether it should exist, for there was general agreement that corruption in rural areas was a problem; the issue was how it should be handled. Mao favored a bottom-up approach that put the burden of investigation and adjudication on peasant associations made up of the local
populace. The emphasis was on "class struggle." Mao's opponents, notably
Liu Shaoqi, the president of the country, wanted the process handled in a
more orderly, controlled fashion, by work teams sent to villages by central
Party authorities. During the two and one-half years of the campaign, the
approach shifted back and forth, depending on which faction had the
upper hand at a particular time. In many villages numerous cadres were*

criticized and lost their positions. Often, when the campaign proceeded along Maoist lines, from the bottom up, it was used as a vehicle for settling personal grudges and clan feuds within villages. The general atmosphere was contentious and divisive.[1] Such was not the case in Houhua Village. There the campaign was relatively mild. Few were disciplined, and none severely. The explanation lies in two factors: First, under Wang Fucheng's leadership there was little corruption in Houhua Village, and second, Wang's highest priority as Party secretary was to maintain unity in the village and address divisive issues before they became serious. In consistently giving priority to unity over struggle, Wang Fucheng was unwittingly at odds with his hero Mao Zedong.

There were numerous other campaigns in those years—too numerous for Wang Fucheng to remember. Most were "emulation campaigns" of one sort or another, in which villages and individuals were encouraged to learn from the advanced experience of others. None had much effect on Houhua Village, according to Wang Fucheng, except to waste time and money.

When I discussed the campaigns of the early 1960s with Wang Fucheng, it was apparent that he had little interest in them and little knowledge of their particulars. That explains the brevity of this chapter. It also illustrates a significant point—in a country as large as China, even the most comprehensive campaigns initiated by an authoritarian government will have diverse results.

Wang Fucheng:

After the Great Leap Forward, there was a campaign to "Counter the Five Winds." Its purpose was mainly to readjust for cadres' past mistakes. Cadres came from outside the village and asked us to organize criticism and struggle meetings, which we did. We reported the activities of village cadres to the outside cadres, and they chose the struggle targets. When we suggested to the outside cadres someone to be struggled against, they generally agreed. Reasons for criticism differed—a cadre stole something, or was lazy, or didn't use a farm animal well. There was seldom public criticism of common people who stole. They were mostly very poor and didn't have enough to eat. We usually educated them individually.

Three cadres in this village were severely criticized. One was the brigade accountant, and another was a team accountant. I don't remember the third one. They were asked to go to the county for special study classes. When they came back, they still held cadre positions.

I was only slightly criticized because I was honest and only did what I thought was right. I hadn't behaved badly. The people said, "Wang Fucheng is a good cadre." Furthermore, my uncle was behind me.

Another campaign at that time was the "Three Togethers Movement." Cadres from the city were sent here to "work together, live together, and eat together" with the peasants. The campaign was supposed to prevent bureaucratism among higher-level cadres and bring them closer to the common people. Those cadres were also supposed to check on our activities. Four were sent here from Anyang City. One was the leader of a newspaper publishing house. I don't recall what the others did. They lived and ate here in ordinary people's homes. Two were in the number-two production team, and two were in number three. The brigade arranged for their meals, but they paid their own expenses. I recall that one was named Li Fucheng. He had a small notebook with the names of all the members of his production team. He went to the houses of all of the members to eat without arrangement by the team leaders.

The cadres had the power to direct our work. Sometimes they went to the commune to report on the situation here. Their power was greater than ours. Sometimes they helped us settle problems. I'll give you an example. Once, the brigade leader and I had a fierce argument. I thought he was trying to overthrow me as Party secretary. I was in charge of political affairs. He told me I should take care of farming. That was his job. To tell you the truth, I wasn't so skillful at farm work. He wanted me to do that job to prove me incapable. I knew that a cadre from the commune named Dong supported him. I was very upset. I didn't say anything to him. I went to the fields and worked day and night on irrigation. Li Fucheng [the outside cadre] saw that my mood was deep and asked me about it. He then said, "Your health is not good. You are not supposed to go to the fields." He went to the commune and reported the whole story. The commune Party secretary [the highest leader] who came to the village to investigate said, "Wang Fucheng is honest and cannot tell a lie." He decided that I should continue to be in charge of Party affairs and that the brigade leader should keep his job. Dong was transferred to another place.

In those years [between the Great Leap Forward and the Cultural Revolution] there were two or three campaigns each year and many, many meetings. There were so many I can't remember them all. The form was always the same. Cadres from the commune and county would come here to organize meetings and give instructions. In Houhua Village, these campaigns were mostly a waste of time and money.

One campaign [in 1964] was to learn from and catch up to others. I traveled to many places to study their experiences. People also came here to observe us. I went to Liuxinggu Village in this county and to Qiliying and Liuzhuang villages in Xinxiang County west of here. I went to Zhengzhou City [the Provincial capital] several times and once to Hua County and to a county east of Shijiazhuang City in Hebei Province to observe their wheat-farming methods. I went to Liuzhuang two or three times and saw that they raised forty to fifty milk cows. That was new to me. They also had two small factories and a machine repair shop and other non-farming occupations that were going very well. They lived in two-story houses. Their fields were managed very well. They went to the fields and came back at fixed times. I introduced everything that I saw to people in our brigade, but we didn't use any of the experiences from the places we visited. We were too backward, and we didn't have enough money. I did not enjoy the travel; it wasted a lot of money from the masses. But I had to go. Once, I was sent to the Tianjin City area, hundreds of miles away, to see how the accountant in a certain village worked. I was upset that the commune cadres sent me because I couldn't read and write, but it was their decision that I should be included in the trip.

There was also a campaign to learn from Lei Feng.[2] It was not very important in this village. It was mainly for the young. We just asked our youth to learn from Lei Feng. I don't remember much about it.

A more important campaign was the "Four Cleanups."[3] It began with a short campaign [the "Small Four Cleanups"] in 1963. The Party sent cadres from outside to check our account books. They asked how much grain we produced, how much we gave to the government, how much to the masses, how the brigade spent its money, and what the current income of the brigade, of cadres, and of ordinary peasants was. Because I had acted honestly, they found no problems with our account books. I was not criticized by the cadres. As I remember, no one in this village was criticized. Here it was a small campaign that lasted a short time.

It was followed by a "Big Four Cleanups" campaign,[4] which lasted longer. There were a lot of problems in many other villages in this district, and many cadres were criticized. I was very busy at that time going to the commune for meetings every three days or so and to the county about once a month. There was only one bicycle in the village then. It belonged to the brigade. I rode it to the meetings. It took an hour and a half to get to Neihuang town. When it rained it took even longer. I sometimes stayed in a guest house in the county town for a few days until the roads were better. Our economic accounts were checked again to see if any money had been wasted or if there had been graft. Because I was illiterate, I had the old accountants check the books of the new ones and report to me. I had spent frugally and had not made any mistakes. The brigade accountant then was Wang Changjun. He was about thirty. He was criticized for wasting funds. When he worked with others he invited them to eat and drink using brigade funds. He didn't graft a lot of money, but he wasted too much. At a mass meeting held to struggle against him, the people said he wasted property that was the blood of poor peasants. They also said he had problems related to sex, but they couldn't find any evidence.

I regard the Four Cleanups as mainly an education campaign. No Party member in this village was driven from the Party at that time. We didn't punish people except, at most, we changed their duties. Wang Changjun was asked to be a team leader rather than an accountant. When we had meetings we seldom mentioned cadres by name because in a village the one thing we should do is build unity. If a cadre made a mistake and we immediately disposed of him, we could not do very well. There were not many people in the village who would be cadres because the people often showed their dissatisfaction with them. Cadres were likely to offend the ordinary people and then get criticized. They didn't get much more money than the ordinary people, but they had to pay more attention to production. Also, sometimes people who are active in campaigns and are judged to be capable leave the village for other occupations. Very few did that here. Only one brigade militia leader went to the county government to be a cadre. Here we have had few leadership problems.

6

"At the Risk of Death, Dare to Throw the Emperor from His Horse": The Great Proletarian Cultural Revolution, 1966–1976

Wang Fucheng became increasingly excited and agitated as he recalled the events of the "Great Proletarian Cultural Revolution" in Houhua Village. At one point his wife came in to ask him to lower his voice because the neighbors were wondering what was going on.

Like most of the rest of the Chinese population, no one in Houhua Village knew what the Cultural Revolution was about when it began in late 1966. Indeed, there is much disagreement to this day about what its purpose was. Some see it as a power struggle, pure and simple, in which Mao Zedong was willing to use any means and sacrifice any number of people to regain the influence he had lost following the Great Leap Forward. Others, while granting the power struggle, see it motivated primarily by crucial differences in ideology. According to this latter perspective, it was primarily an effort by Party Chairman Mao Zedong to achieve what he had been unable to achieve in the Socialist Education Campaign—he wanted to revive the revolutionary spirit of collectivism and class struggle and imbue that spirit in untutored youth by using them as the vehicle to topple Party elites who were "taking the bourgeois road." Mao put special emphasis on culture because it was there, in the realm of thought, that the pernicious remnants of "capitalism" and "feudalism" continued to flourish—political and economic institutions had become socialist, but people's ideas had not. The old culture, both ideas and material objects, were to be smashed, and all leadership was to be subjected to the test of mass criticism.

One thing that all who have analyzed the Cultural Revolution agree on is that the direction it took was not planned. Events unfolded chaotically as people sought to interpret Chairman Mao's vague pronouncements. Many people took advantage of the general breakdown of order to settle old scores or to seek power. Factional strife, largely undefined by substantive issues, became the principal manifestation of the "revolution" at the grassroots level. Tens of thousands of people were killed, and according to an estimate by Mao's successor, Deng Xiaoping, 2.9 million people were unjustly persecuted. Many estimates are higher. Following Mao's death in 1976, the Communist Party of China condemned the Cultural Revolution as an unmitigated disaster and laid the blame on Mao himself.

Wang Fucheng was loath to criticize Mao for anything, but he too could find nothing good to say about those years. In Houhua Village, they were characterized by largely meaningless criticism and intra-village conflict, but Houhua was unusual in that there was no physical violence; and it was the first of the twenty-two villages in the commune to reestablish stability and order, bringing an end to the first phase of the Cultural Revolution. Few Party secretaries in the area had survived the ordeal with their power intact. Wang Fucheng was an exception.

Wang Fucheng:

In mid-1966 I was called to the county seat for several days and told that another campaign had come. The main purpose, I was told, was to struggle against those in power, and the main target was to be the Party secretary. They said, "You should mobilize the masses, and you yourself will be the struggle target. If you don't hold a meeting in your village, it will show that you have a lot of problems."

After I returned from the county I held a meeting first with the Party members in the village. I told them that a "cultural revolution" had started. I actually didn't know the significance of it myself, but I made it clear to the cadres that they should speak out about their own problems, such as graft, illicit sex, and any other illegal activities.

I then held a village meeting to transmit the spirit of the county meeting. I said, "I am the number-one person in power. The village head is second. You should criticize us." The team leaders were not considered to be in power then, so there was no struggle against them at that time, but later there was.

Wang Changmin was also called to the county to help organize the village for struggle. He can tell you about it.

Wang Changmin continues the account:

I was called to the county meeting along with Wang Fucheng. I was director of the Poor Peasants Representative Association [formed during the

Wang Changmin (left), leader of the Eight Twenty-three faction during the Cultural Revolution, and Wang Fucheng (1987).

Big Four Cleanups campaign to help investigate cadres]. At the county meeting we were told why there had to be a "cultural revolution" and how to carry it out. They wanted us to organize the masses to struggle against "bourgeois thought." That term had many meanings, but generally it meant anything opposed to current Party policy. We were also told that the masses should overthrow those currently holding power. I was instructed to mobilize the masses because I was the poor peasants' representative. I didn't have anything against Wang Fucheng or the village head, Wang Zhangyin. In fact, I had introduced both of them to the Party when I was Party secretary myself back in the 1950s. I gave up the position, and Wang Fucheng took over, because I was in poor health. When the Cultural Revolution started, I was the accountant for the fourth production team. After mobilizing the peasants as instructed by the county officials, I withdrew from the organizing committee because I too was a leader. Later I reluctantly became the head of one of the factions in the village, the Eight Twenty-three [see later]. I was asked many times to join Eight Twenty-three and refused. Finally I joined because I wanted to help prevent fighting here. There was a lot of fighting in other villages in this area, but we never actually came to blows in Houhua.

Wang Fucheng continues:

Wang Changmin and I were not in the same faction. I wasn't in any faction. I myself was a faction. At the first struggle meeting I was very upset. After all, I was the Party secretary. No one had ever dared to argue with me before. The people at the first meeting were all from the village. No one came from outside. They told me to stand in front of the table. I asked if I should stand beside the table. They said, "No, in front." They criticized me and didn't let me speak. I just had to listen. I was not severely criticized because most of us are in the same Wang family here. People did not hate me. I was much better off than cadres elsewhere who had to stand bent forward with their arms behind their back in an airplane position.

After the meeting the people paraded in the streets and shouted slogans for several days. In some places cadres were badly beaten. I wasn't ever hit, but the village head, Wang Zhengyin, was. People slapped him during the demonstration. They said he was not frank and honest and that he should be deprived of his rights. I myself turned power over to the militia leader. I was out of power for nearly two years. Meanwhile I became a group leader for production.

The brigade system was abolished at that time, and many people sought power. Anyone with ability could get power. If someone set up a flag and said, "Who will follow me?" he might draw supporters. Several were successful. Eventually there were two factions: One was called the Red Guards, and the other was called Eight Twenty-three, signifying the date, August 23, 1966, that it had broken with the Red Guard group, which had been formed first. Seventy percent of the villagers were in the Red Guards, but it too had subfactions.

In the beginning, some felt that those who had held power and been cadres should be allowed to join. Others disagreed. There were a lot of arguments. Eventually the Red Guard group was chosen by the head of the organization, Zhang Minshou. Many were not allowed to join because they were said to be former landlords or rich peasants, backward or lazy people, and troublemakers. Many of those people later joined Eight Twenty-three. The heads of these organizations were mostly older people, not youths. The two groups each had their own seal of authority.[1] The factions were not based on family in this village. People who shared opinions joined together.

Although I was no longer Party secretary I was still a cadre and was frequently required to go to meetings at the commune and county headquarters. Back in the village I told the two groups what I had learned at the meetings and assigned them tasks. At the same time, I was often struggled against by them. This went on for months. In the daytime the Red Guards struggled against me. The Eight Twenty-three struggled against me in the evening. Each day I had to report my activities to the two leaders. They had the power, the seals, the flags. I told them that I would arrive at their meetings on time. I decided that whatever they asked me to confess, I would, if I had done it. Otherwise I wouldn't. Even if they cursed me and called me *bahuitou* [one who has sex with his son-in-law] I would not retort with even one word.

I was accused of abusively using about 100 yuan [1 yuan = US$.50 at the time] of brigade money when cadres from other villages had visited us. I had invited them to eat watermelons in the field. Some people thought that because I had joined in the eating I should pay the brigade back. I did pay back some money.

In another case, our village had bought some coal. We distributed it to the masses, and they paid for it. They asked why I shouldn't pay for the coal that I used if they had to pay for theirs. They said I had misused public funds. I finally did pay some money.

I regarded some of their accusations to be reasonable and some not. Some said that the medicine that I took was paid for by the commune only because I was a cadre. They said I had a "wide face" [status and prestige] because of my position. The medicine taken by other people was not paid for by the government, so I should pay the money back. That was nonsense. I didn't pay anything back. I was also accused of misusing my authority to distribute grain arbitrarily, and of wrongly using my power to promote cadres. These words were incorrect, but I could only listen.

In these struggle meetings, some people supported me and some didn't. There was a lot of disagreement, especially between the Eight Twenty-three faction and the Red Guard faction. They each began to treat me very differently and to argue with each other about the struggle against me. Once, I was told to go to the Eight Twenty-three headquarters late at night. When the Red Guards and masses heard this, they came and demanded to know why this struggle was being called so late at night. "Do you intend to kill Wang Fucheng?" they asked. They all started shouting and cursing, "You dirty crossbreeds in a basket." Finally I was set free. The next day, the arguments were even more fierce.

Another time, the Red Guards and Eight Twenty-three argued in front of my gate. A large crowd gathered. I carried several tables and stools from the school and asked the two factions to stand on either side. I said, "You may argue but not fight. Remember Chairman Mao's words, 'Fight with words, not with weapons.'" They agreed, but the argument got heated and they were about to fight. I climbed up on the roof of my house. There were two reasons for doing that. One, I was afraid they would think I backed one side, and the other side would beat me. The other reason was that I wanted to see which side started the fight and if anyone was badly beaten. I shouted, "Struggle with words, not with weapons. I will see who fights first." I was a cadre, after all, so they didn't fight, but they continued to curse each other. Later, when I told this story to the commune cadres, they all laughed at me for being too timid. But in many villages the people fought day and night using spears, big knives, and manure forks.

In 1968 the government asked us to form a Revolutionary Committee[2] and restore order. For two months that was impossible. The arguments were too heated. When they calmed down a bit, I had a chance to speak. I said, "You have struggled against me a lot, but I do not have a low opinion of you. Now I want to say something to you. If you feel that what I say is right, please listen; if wrong, you can continue to struggle against me." I said: "You are all false revolutionaries! Why? You have fought and argued every day when Chairman Mao has asked us to unify. Why not follow Chairman Mao's words?" There was still no response to my call. Both sides had their own seal of power. The brigade seal had been set aside long ago. In the following days I tried my best to convince them to unify. At another meeting I asked the leaders of both organizations if either of them came from landlord or rich peasant families. They both said no, so I asked why poor and lower-middle[3] peasants should shout at each other day and night. I asked them to give me their seals, for I was an old cadre in the village and the commune cadres had asked me to convince them to stop arguing. I said, "Those who hand me their power seal are revolutionaries. Those who don't are counterrevolutionaries." The Red Guards agreed. Eight Twenty-three said they would think about it. Two days later, at another meeting, Eight Twenty-three agreed to give up their seal if the other side confessed that the argument was their fault. I said, "In the past, I was responsible for all of the faults in the brigade. You may pour your criticisms on me, but one thing is certain, you should give me the seal." The next day they brought it to me. Later I gave the two seals to the brigade accountant to keep. I then suggested that a brigade Revolutionary Committee be formed. They agreed, and the leaders of the two factions and all of the masses elected me director. I was in power again.

The Revolutionary Committee in our village was the first in this area. The commune cadres gathered cadres from the other twenty-one villages in the commune, and all of them, over one hundred, came here to learn from us. Houhua became a model for other villages. I made a speech saying we should listen to Chairman Mao's call to unify. We should pay attention to farm work and fight no more. I showed the two power seals, and all applauded. Later there was another meeting in the commune calling on all of the commune population to learn from Houhua Village. Soon, Revolutionary Committees were established throughout the commune. Not long after that, we began to rebuild the Party organization. All agreed that Wang Fucheng was the person to be Party secretary in Houhua Village. I was then concurrently director of the Revolutionary Committee and Party secretary.

Study the Thoughts of Chairman Mao

During the Cultural Revolution everyone studied the words of Chairman Mao. I went to the commune to study, and the commune trained study instructors for our village. There were seven study instructors, one for each team and one for the whole brigade. We bought a lot of red treasure books of Chairman Mao's sayings and distributed them to the villagers. We all tried to learn the quotations by heart. I remembered only those I found useful. The others I forgot quickly. I never could learn the "Three Venerable Articles"[4] by heart.

Some of Chairman Mao's words were helpful in our work, but there were a lot we couldn't use. Today I can remember only two quotations: "At the risk of death, dare to throw the Emperor from his horse" and "What is work? Work is struggle. Wherever there is struggle, there we must go. We go to settle problems; the more difficult the problem, the more we should want to go." That second quotation was the most useful to us cadres. Why? Because we exist to solve problems. If we don't go where there are problems and try to solve them, why should we exist?

We had a picture of Chairman Mao in our house, and everyone wore a badge with Chairman Mao on it. We have thrown them all away now. If cadres made mistakes, they were supposed to confess before Chairman Mao's picture; then they were allowed to eat supper. I don't remember ever doing that myself. But we all did hold our red books in our hands and shout many times, "Ten thousand years to Chairman Mao! Ten thousand, ten thousand years to you! Our beloved Chairman Mao, sun of our hearts, Chairman Mao!" We also sang songs to Chairman Mao. I don't remember the words now.

There were two or three study campaigns a year. I don't remember them all. I was illiterate, so I said the slogans and then forgot them. The study instructors helped the villagers learn something about them. Mostly, young people took part in the study meetings. We participated on the demand of the commune government. I do remember shouting, "Down with Lin Biao and Kong's second son [Kong lao er—Confucius]." I really don't know who Confucius was. Was he a big capitalist? I heard that he was a big capitalist and a landlord from Shandong Province. There were several generations of ancestors in his family. He didn't take part in manual labor because he was a big landlord and capitalist. Some village leaders went to visit his living place. There was no relationship between that campaign and our production.

Lin Biao was vicechairman of the Communist Party but later betrayed the Party. He tried to seize power from Chairman Mao. When he failed, he escaped in an airplane and crashed in the Soviet Union.[5] The villagers thought the plane crash served him right. I did, too. He just pretended to back Chairman Mao. I have seen pictures of him. Whenever he appeared with Chairman Mao, he stood behind him. He always had the red book. He seemed to be listening to Chairman Mao's words, but his heart had already become evil. The masses knew he was bad. He was a very short, monkey-like person. His face looked just like a monkey's. Later, when we argued with people, we called them "Lin Biao." Lin Biao was a bad egg, and no one wanted to be a bad egg.

Was there a campaign here to criticize Chen Boda [Chairman Mao's former secretary and chief ideological adviser]? I never heard of him. Is he a high-level cadre from Zhengzhou?[6]

"Learn from Dazhai"

I had to spend a lot of time in those years going to other places to study their experiences. I went three times to Dazhai, the model brigade in Shanxi Province, in response to Chairman Mao's call, "In agriculture, learn from Dazhai."[7] Dazhai is 1,000 li from here. The trip takes two days, but usually it took us seven or eight because we had to gather many cadres together from nearby villages. We had to rent buses and trucks to go to the county seat and then to Anyang, where we would take the train. Often we would stop in Luoyang or Zhengzhou for a few days. The whole trip, going and coming back, took seven to fifteen days and cost several hundred yuan. The government gave us no money. We had to use funds from the brigade. It was mostly a big waste of time and money. Many cadres from here didn't want to go, but the commune and county government kept urging us to learn from the Dazhai experience. They called us backward and asked why we shouldn't go. So the team cadres discussed it and decided they had to go even though it wasted several hundred yuan from the villagers.

As many as 70,000–80,000 people visited Dazhai at a time. Some came from as far away as 6,000 li. They had to live in Xiyang county seat and all the surrounding towns. All of the hotels and guest houses were full. Some city people had to give up their own rooms to the visitors.

So-called visiting Dazhai was just walking around the mountains one time and then going to Xiyang county seat and staying for several days. That ended our visit. There were no interviews with Dazhai cadres. They were too busy. If we asked the brigade members questions, they just told us to watch for ourselves. They couldn't answer our questions.

We didn't think the Dazhai model was valuable for us. The village is smaller than ours. It is in a mountain area; here it is flat. They plant mostly corn and sorghum and harvest only once a year. We plant many crops and harvest twice. We didn't think they were any better off than we were. We never did adopt their work-point system.[8] The only thing I think was better there is that the villagers had two-story buildings. We didn't have those. I was also impressed that the rooms in the villagers' houses were very clean. But I didn't think Dazhai and Xiyang County were better than here. So when people asked for a comparison I told them, "Yes, I have gone to see Dazhai. I just watched, that's all." I was disappointed with Dazhai, but I dared not say so at that time.

I was very excited when I saw the Lin County irrigation project [the celebrated Red Flag Canal]. They must have used a lot of effort to build that. But it wasn't useful for this area.

We also had a local model to learn from. It was the Double Tranquility Commune, about eighteen li from here, beyond Jingdian market town. It had about thirty brigades. One of them was also called Dazhai. I visited that Dazhai and two other key villages, Huzhuang and Huagu, often. I went to Huzhuang at least four times. Their output was higher than ours. If we got 300 jin per mu, they would get 500. Their crop planting was better than ours. They would alternate crops in different fields, and they planted various kinds of trees. They had a lot of enthusiasm. I would tell our villagers to learn from them, but it was not easy. For instance, we tried to introduce their pig-feeding methods. Their brigade raised pigs scientifically in one area. We raised them in each team. When we copied them, we seemed to be succeeding at first, but then we failed because we didn't have enough feed. I think they might have had help from the government. I figure they did get better treatment from the government because they were models for others to follow. They could buy machines like tractors and pumps more easily than other places. Also, the government may have supplied them with more fertilizer.

But I'll tell you, later there were great changes there. The contradictions between the cadres and the masses came out suddenly during the Cultural Revolution. People cursed each other and fought. They divided into different factions, each backed by different cadres. There were problems of confused accounts and graft. The commune changed the cadres many times, but the problems couldn't be solved. Almost all the land was wasted, and almost all the trees were cut down to be sold. The village was out of control. Today it is still a backward village. It is in the lowest category of villages, the third.[9] The people cannot even afford to pay taxes to the government.

In 1974 we were asked to learn from another model near Tianjin City called Xiaojinzhuang. It was being promoted by Jiang Qing, Chairman Mao's wife. The study instructor told our youth about it, but I paid no attention. Officials from the commune said, "Wang Fucheng, you have rightist tendencies in your thought. If you want to catch up with other villages, why not learn from Xiaojinzhuang?" I replied that there are many advanced experiences in our own county. Why not learn from them? We had too many models to learn from at that time. It was a waste of time and money. Our main purpose was to raise the standard of living of our own village and to make more contributions to the country. It didn't matter a lot if we learned from Xiaojinzhuang. I never did go.

Educated Youth "Up to the Mountains, Down to the Villages"

At about that same time, I think it was 1973, some educated youth from the city settled in this village. Chairman Mao had said, "Educated youth should go up to the mountains and down to the villages to be reeducated by the poor and lower-middle peasants." There were thirty-two of them. Ten were girls. All were from from Anyang City. They came only to this village and Liuxinggu Village because conditions were better here than in most other villages in the area.

When they came, we enthusiastically welcomed them with fireworks. A cadre from the city came with them. I was going to hold a meeting for him and the educated youth, but when I heard some of them say they would beat me first and the city cadre second, we canceled the meeting. Still, at the beginning, some of them seemed very determined. They said they would stay in the villages for their whole lives. We built new buildings for them with over twenty rooms. The villagers did not like having them here. They said they ate but did nothing but idle around. I met with the villagers and said, "We must heed the Party's call." I also said, "Their parents aren't here. We should take care of them." When some of them argued with me, I cursed them: "You turtle's grandson"[turtle's son is a colloquial expression for "bastard" in China]. I knew that sometimes I overcriticized the villagers to try to build unity with the students.

The students quarreled all day long among themselves. Some fought each other continually. When they wanted to fight the villagers, the villagers walked away and avoided the fight. Some obeyed the cadres, some didn't. They worked in each team along with the villagers and were evaluated by them for work points. They didn't get many work points because they didn't work hard. Sometimes their parents came to see them and brought them things. They began to go back to Anyang frequently, and some didn't come back. Some found work in the cities, and some joined the army. Finally there were only three left. I don't remember when they, too, finally left. We were glad to get rid of them. They were a burden to us. They made trouble, and we had nothing in common. I spent half of my energy dealing with them. My greatest disappointment in all my years as a cadre was my failure to create unity between those educated youths and the villagers.

In addition to those educated youths, we were sometimes visited by "sent-down cadres."[10] They were sent to learn from us and to lead study and farm production. Mostly they just came from the commune. They didn't live here long. In general they visited backward brigades more and well-run brigades less. We didn't have to rely on them to settle problems here.

The Cultural Revolution came to an end when Chairman Mao died in 1976. Earlier that year, Premier Zhou Enlai died. We learned of it from the radio. We held a meeting to discuss the news. All of the masses soon knew about it. We all felt deep grief. The masses all knew that Premier Zhou had made great contributions to the country and had devoted his whole life to the revolutionary cause. They felt that they themselves had lost a leader and that it was a great pity that he had left no children. We heard that the premier's body was burned and his ashes were scattered in the rivers, but we didn't know whether to believe this.[11] We thought he should have left children behind because he had worked for the Party and the country for decades.

We heard about Chairman Mao's death on the radio, too. We knew that there were a lot of leaders around his bed when he took his last breath. We also knew when he went to Eight Treasures Mountain to be buried.[12] We had a memorial meeting in the village. Many of the old cadres cried. I also cried. Some of the young people didn't. We cried because of grief, not because we were told to. We thought about what Chairman Mao had given us—land, an end to banditry, a happy life.

7

Houhua Village After Mao: Prosperity and Future Prospects, 1977–1990

In the aftermath of the Cultural Revolution, following the death of Mao Zedong in 1976, dramatic changes took place throughout China. In the early 1980s rural enterprises and institutions were decollectivized, and a "responsibility system" was introduced. In this chapter, Wang Fucheng, the village doctor, and the accountant explain the process of transition from collectivity to responsibility in Houhua Village and the operation of the new system in agriculture, medicine, and education. They also discuss changes in the land and other reasons for rapid increases in production and greatly enhanced prosperity in Houhua Village during the 1980s.

Wang Fucheng was a reluctant convert to the policy of decollectivization. He had worked hard to establish the cooperative system in the 1950s and felt that it had served the village well. Houhua gave it up later than most other villages, and even when production rose under the responsibility system, Wang Fucheng clung to the notion that collectivization had been desirable in its time. It is probably not a coincidence that Wang Fucheng retired as Party secretary in 1984, the year that decollectivization was accomplished, though he claims that the two events were not related. His whole career had been dedicated to implementing the policies of Mao Zedong. When Mao's policies were replaced by those of his successors, it was a suitable time for Wang Fucheng to step down.

Wang Fucheng's comments on land redistribution, the responsibility system, and the village brick kiln in this chapter were made in interviews that I conducted in 1989 and 1990. Readers will notice when reading Chapter 10 that by 1994 the situation with regard to all of these things had changed considerably. The village, like the rest of China, is in a state of continual transition.

The prices mentioned in this chapter were those in effect in 1990. At that time, US$1 = 5 yuan, approximately.

Wang Fucheng:

Did we benefit at all from the Cultural Revolution? No. Nothing good had come of it, and many cadres had suffered a lot. It was hard for them to be paraded around in tall hats and have a board hung in front of them announcing their supposed crimes.

There have been a lot of changes since then. The most important was the end of collective farming and the introduction of the "responsibility system." We were late in doing that here. We didn't do it until after the fall 1984 harvest. Other brigades in this area did it one or two years before us. We thought we were better than others, so we would wait and see. We had a problem with our thinking at that time.

The poor villages adopted it first because they weren't doing so well and thought they could do better. We visited them after the first year and saw that they did do better than before, so we adopted the new system at the end of 1983. But even then, for another year, we didn't divide up property as the government asked. We continued to plow and irrigate the land collectively and didn't redistribute tools and animals. We just asked individual families to take care of a share of land. We were afraid of the consequences of losing the property and equipment of the brigade. Later we were deeply influenced by the success of other villages, and also by some cadres from outside who persuaded us to adopt the responsibility system. We lost some income we should have had in the two years we continued to use the old collective system.

In dividing the land, each team first measured its land and put it into categories of good, not-so-good, and bad. We then determined comparable shares and assigned a number to each share and put it on a piece of paper. Peasants' representatives watched us do that. In determining how much each household got, we also took into account the number of members in the household. We then had a blind drawing. There were a lot of arguments—"this isn't fair, that isn't fair." It was difficult to divide the land equitably. There were fields near and far from the village, good land and bad land. We held many meetings to discuss and explain the division and make readjustments. In 1986 we did the whole thing over again because there were so many complaints. Now we have decided to have a new division every ten years. The land is still all owned collectively by the village. The individual households only manage it for a fixed period of time.

We divided the farm animals by evaluating the worth of each animal, adding the value of all of them to get their total worth, and then dividing that number by the number of people in the whole village. For instance, the total value of the animals might be 50 yuan per person and perhaps 300 yuan per household. We then attached to the animal a sheet of paper with its value written on it. Household representatives then drew for them. If the value of the animal was higher than the household allotment, they might share it with other households. Households that didn't get an animal or didn't get their full share were then paid comparable amounts by the households that did get animals or whose animals were worth more than their allotment. Tools, carts, tractors, and other equipment were divided up in the same way. Over the next several years the contents of storehouses—even the storehouses themselves—all of the property of the brigade and the teams, were distributed. Machines for processing cotton and grinding grain were bought from the brigade by individual households. They now charge a fee for their use and keep the money for themselves.

The orchards were divided by lot in a blind drawing by those who wanted them instead of other land. Households responsible for them had to give 40 yuan per mu to the village for the first three years they had the orchard plot and 10 yuan more each year for the ten years they manage it. After ten years the orchards will be redistributed along with all the other land. When we expanded the orchards at government request two years ago, they were managed by those who already had responsibility for the land. During the years that the trees are maturing and produce no fruit, the management households get no compensation and they pay no tax to the village. They still do all right because it is only about 10 percent of their land.

An irrigation system for the land was dug when there was collective farming and was paid for by the brigade. Each family now pays for the electricity to pump water for its own fields. There is an electricity meter for each household and for all equipment. The amount each family pays for electricity differs. A man is in charge of the whole electric system. Our family of seven pays about 300 yuan per year. About 15 percent of that is for household use, and the rest is for farming.

A large brick kiln built by the brigade is now under private management, too. Six families got together and invested 30,000 yuan to pay the village for the kiln proper, the chimney, the brick-making machine, and wheelbarrows. Some of the money was their own, and some they borrowed from a bank. They have responsibility for the brick-making operation for five years. The first year of their investment they paid nothing more to the village, but the second year they paid 10,000 yuan; the third year, 20,000 yuan; the fourth, 30,000; and the fifth, 40,000. The amount is decided by the village leaders. This is the fifth year. There will be a new contract for the next five years. The village leaders will determine a new fee schedule. The kiln is running very well now. It can fire 10,000 bricks at a time. The bricks

Harvesting wheat. Most wheat harvesting is still done with hand knives rather than with a scythe as is shown here.

are made simply by mixing water with the local soil in a mold, drying it, and then firing. Having the kiln has made it cheap to rebuild our houses. Many villagers also make money hauling the bricks on donkey carts to other locations. The bricks are sold in many places—Neihuang county seat, Jingdian, and other market towns—but most are used here in this village. Even though most families here have already built new houses in the past several years, the kiln will be kept busy; now that people have more money, they are concerned with fashion. They will build new houses just to keep up with fashion. In a village, after people have enough to eat, the first thing they think about is their houses.

Village people estimate that each of the six families managing the kiln is making 30,000 yuan per year. I think it is closer to 10,000 to 20,000 yuan, but that is still much more than households earn from farming. It is certain that other families will try to seize management power. It will depend on which group will agree to the village fee request. They themselves might even suggest an amount above the set fee to be donated to the village. There is bound to be a struggle.[1]

The land set aside for the brick kiln was 150 mu. Only about half of it is occupied by the kiln and the soil from which the bricks are made. The rest was divided into almost 100 parcels and distributed to households by blind drawing. There will be another drawing in five years. Those who did not get land in the drawing get no compensation, but the amount of land is so small there is not much quarreling.

Medical services in the village are also under the household responsibility system now. Each household pays all of its own medical expenses. We used to have a collective medical system. Wang Tongjun, one of the village doctors, can tell you about it.

Wang Tongjun:

Until 1958 there was no medical care in this village to speak of. After liberation [1949], there had been some hygiene campaigns to clean manure out of the streets and educate the masses to prevent contagious diseases by cleaning their houses and clothes more frequently, but there were no medical workers or facilities for people who got sick. Then, during the Great Leap Forward [1958], the government set up three "combined clinics" for the twenty-two villages in the commune. One of those clinics was here in Houhua. The clinic had four doctors who served several villages. Treatment was free, but people paid for medicine. Actually, there was almost no medicine. We used local herbal prescriptions that had been handed down through the generations. That clinic lasted until 1969, when, during the Cultural Revolution, we went to a collective medical system. This village (brigade) was the first one in the commune to set up a collective medical system and its own clinic. The brigade contributed 1,000 yuan and built a new building. People paid 0.5 yuan [about US$.25 at the time] a year and then got free medical care. The clinic was staffed by two "barefoot doctors."[2] I was one of them. I was nineteen at the time and had a junior secondary school education. My only medical training had been working with the medical workers in the combined clinic. As a barefoot doctor, I went to the commune clinic each year for a month of training. We still had almost no medicine, so we concentrated on prevention. For instance, in winter we told people to drink water boiled with ginger and onions to prevent colds and to breathe steamed vinegar if they had congestion. We also used loudspeakers and wrote slogans on the wall to educate people about hygiene. There was a hygiene campaign called "two controls, five transformations"—control water and manure; transform latrines, stoves, animal yards and stables, streets, and water sources.

Our clinic was considered the most advanced in the whole commune and even in the whole county. Still, medical care was inadequate. The barefoot doctor system never worked very well. People complained a lot. The 0.5 yuan per year that they paid was not enough to buy medicine or equipment. The barefoot doctors received work points no matter how well or poorly they performed. Today our income depends on how we run our private clinics. When the responsibility system began, I went to the county hospital for a year for training. There is still no fee for the doctor's services; people pay only for medicine. I buy the medicine in Jingdian market town. I make a 15 percent profit on it. Most of it is Western medicine, but some people still want Chinese medicine. I use acupuncture a lot for chronic diseases.

The profit from my medical practice last year [1989] was 1,500 yuan. Our household also has ten mu of farmland that is cultivated mostly by my oldest son and his wife, but we all work on it during the busy seasons. Our total income for our household of six people was 9,000 yuan.

Wang Fucheng continues:

Even though people now pay medical fees themselves they prefer the current system. The medical care is much better, and they can afford the extra cost. If there are serious problems, they can go to the township clinic or the county hospital. They usually have to pay the fees there, too. For really big problems, like cancer, people go to a big city hospital, if they can afford it and if they can get in. Often you need special connections to be admitted to a city hospital. To pay the bills, people will try to borrow from relatives. If they cannot pay, they just stay home. There is no national health system. The government pays medical costs only for government employees.

About ten years ago there was a case of a seven-year-old child whose leg was cut off by a tractor from Jingdian. He was sent to the Jingdian clinic. The unit that owned the tractor paid for everything. He was also given 500 yuan compensation, but no arrangements were made concerning his later life. Now that he is an adult he has no way to make a living. He has gone here and there telling his story and trying to get help. The director of the district People's Representative Assembly in Anyang asked the county officials to solve his problem, but they said that the accident was long ago and there is no solution now. His family has to take care of him.

Wang Shuanglan, the village accountant:

I'll give you an example of the normal cost for medical care now. Two days ago I had a cold. I went to the doctor and spent 2 yuan for medicine. The income for my household last year was about 4,000 yuan, including the amount we spent for farming investment this year. There are nine members of the household. Five can do physical labor. We spend, on average, about 200 yuan on medical care if there is no serious illness in the family. That is about 5 percent of our income.

Wang Fucheng continues:

The cost of education in the village is also mainly the responsibility of those whose children are in school. A household pays 30 yuan tuition for each child in school. That includes books and all fees. The village as a whole paid for new school buildings in 1984. There was a special collection for that of 20 yuan per household. That is not much. Everyone could afford

Village school and children (1990).

it. Also, if necessary, the village can support education with the tax money it collects from the kiln and orchards.

Before the new school was built, education in this village was not very good. We used the old family temple as a school until the Cultural Revolution. In the temple there were two classrooms in which five grades were taught simultaneously by two or three teachers. Only about 60 percent of the village children attended classes, and many of them came intermittently. There was no regularity. During the Cultural Revolution we built five new classrooms where the new school now stands. More children came to school then, but there was a lot of disruption in those days and school was not run on a regular basis.

Our new school is what is called a "popular management, public help" school. The teachers are paid both by the village [through tuition] and the state. There are three categories of teachers in the school: those whose salary is paid completely by the state, those whose salary is paid half by the state and half by the village, and those whose salary is paid completely by the village. Of the nine teachers in the school, two are in the first category, five are in the second category, and two are in the third category. Those paid by the state have the highest salaries; one earns 120 yuan per month, the other 100 yuan. Three of the teachers in the second category, those paid by the state and the village, make 60 yuan per month each, and two make 50 yuan. The other two teachers, who are paid only by the village, make 50 yuan. Those in the second and third categories also have land allotments, which their family members work with their help in the busy season and other times when school is not in session. The village can add as many teachers in the third category as it wishes to pay. Almost 100 percent of the children in this village now finish primary school, and most go on to junior secondary school.

When the responsibility system first began, in 1984, there were lots of ways of fixing responsibility for production. In this village, the brigade leaders decided on a fair production amount for each allotment of land. If those responsible for the land produced extra, we gave them more money. If they didn't meet the quota, we fined them. Now [in 1990] the system works differently. The only contract is with the government. The villagers sell a certain amount of grain to the government at lower than market price. The rest they sell to the government at a higher price, or they sell it on the open market to individuals who need grain for their own use. Private commercial trading in grain is not allowed. Only the government can do that. Sometimes the government price is higher, and sometimes the market price is higher. In 1988 we had to sell 180 jin of wheat per person to the government at 26 fen [cents] per jin. In 1989 it was 190 jin per person. That fulfilled the contract; that was our tax. It amounted to about 25 yuan per person. The rest we sold at about 40 fen per jin.

The government, for its side of the contract, sells a certain amount of fertilizer and cooking oil to the households at a very low price. Last year, for every 100 kg of grain, the government sold 10 kg of fertilizer and 5 kg of oil at a price below market value. The production per head averages 900–1,000 jin of grain, so the tax is paid on less than 20 percent of production. The tax is not reduced if people are poor or sick, though they might get other help.

There is a special products tax for the orchards. Cotton is not taxed, but corn is, so more and more of our land is planted in cotton for our second harvest, about 80 percent now.

I'll give you an example of how the system works. Last year my family of seven produced 7,000 jin of grain. We sold 1,260 jin to the government at 26 fen per jin, and 2,000 jin to the government at the market price of about 40 fen per jin. The rest, 3,740 jin, we kept to eat and for seed.

We sell most of our grain at Liucun Township. Sometimes people who need grain bring a cart here to buy it, but usually we take it ourselves, mostly in animal carts. Some people have small, two-wheel tractors. There are sixteen or seventeen in the village. The tractor owners usually don't transport for other people for a fee. If they help others, it is usually relatives, and they do it free. Sometimes people with tractors will charge others about 6 yuan per mu for plowing their fields.

So, basically, under the responsibility system each household looks out for itself. There are only four families in the village that can't do that. We call them Five Guarantees Households.[3] The village leaders collect a special fee for them. They are given 500 jin of wheat, 100 jin of corn, and 10 jin of cooking oil per year, plus 5 yuan cash per month. They don't pay for medical care. Since 1988 Liucun Township has had a "courtyard for nourishing the old" where impoverished old people can go if there is no one in the village to care for them.

Under the new system the people work harder and they get more. They can go to the fields when they wish and plant whatever they wish. They are more likely to spend more time in the fields and are more willing to pay for more fertilizer. Production has increased. Some say that it was easier under the collective system, that they work too hard, are more tired, feel more pressure, and have less security now. But people are basically satisfied and don't think of going back. Since the masses want the new system, I'm in favor of it, too.

But I don't think we could have gone right to the household responsibility system after land reform and skipped collectivization. There had to be a whole process. The process educated people. Right after land reform the struggle of different opinions was very sharp. People viewed the world differently. There were still a lot of bandits and Guomindang troops everywhere. The Communist Party didn't have firm control; people began to sell their land. The government wasn't powerful enough to prevent that. Collectivization was a way to keep the poor from losing their land. Some people didn't want to join the collectives. As for me, I thought it right to develop from a low to a high level of collective farming. I can see that each stage in the process was an attempt to find the best way to build socialism. The whole purpose is to build a socialist country. Why else did the People's Liberation Army lose so many lives in the war? Now, in this stage, the responsibility system is the best way because the people favor it. In this system, the land has still not been removed from collective ownership. No land can be sold without special permission from the government.

There are now some suggestions among the masses that villagers be allowed to rent their land allotments to others for money or grain and then go out buying and selling or take other occupations. We are not yet at that stage. Conditions are not yet right for it in this village. We don't have the money to build a factory, like a cotton-processing plant. The young people here do not have the experience or technical skills to do trading or other occupations. Most of them stay here in the village. We are farmers. That's what we know. There are several tens of households that engage at least part time in occupations other than farming: Six run the brick kiln, four run a kiln for making roof tiles, four process cotton part time—including pressing cotton seeds for oil—nine operate flour mills part time, and many engage in transporting bricks to other locations in their spare time. There are also one government store[4] and four small private stores in the village. These are mostly sideline occupations. I don't think there will be any major changes in the economy of the village soon. We are not near a city or a big river. Our future depends on agriculture, not commerce. If agriculture continues to develop, there will be prosperity.

The great improvement in agricultural production that has given us a much better life recently is not due solely to adoption of the responsibility system. It is the result of a process that began at least two decades before that when we began to convert our salt land to crop land and started irrigating our fields.

Originally, about 1,500 of the 4,000 mu of land in this village was salt land. No crops could be produced on it. Not even grass would grow there. Most of the villagers made and sold salt to help them get by. Now there is no salt, and the land is very productive. In about 1964 we began to get rid of the salt by digging ditches. When it rained, salt came to the surface and then washed into the ditches. Water from the ditches flowed into the Nitrate River, which had been dredged in 1957 to make it flow more easily into the Wei River. We also dug wells and irrigated the land, which washed the salt out. The wells here used to be 7–8 meters deep and were dug by hand. In the 1970s, with the help of the county, we began using drilling machines to dig tube wells 40–50 meters deep. That lowered the water table and also the salt and alkaline level. That is the main reason why salt is no longer a big problem. Then we planted willow trees and huai trees [a kind of locust]. The salt was absorbed by their roots. The trees grew very quickly and very well. They were so thick that people from other villages asked if we had wolves in our forest. After about ten years we cut all of the trees down and cleared the land. Some team cadres even cried then, and some called us *baijiazi* [the son who ruins the family, i.e., prodigal son]. We benefited a lot from those trees. We used the wood in our houses. Then we planted cotton on the land. The government didn't help with money, but agricultural technicians brought in different cotton seeds to test those best for our salt land. The cotton didn't grow well at first because we listened to the technicians and planted it too densely. Later we planted less densely, and output increased. Today that land produces cotton as well as or better than the non-salt land. It is not as good for wheat. We plant wheat there only once in three years.

On 150 mu of the former salt land we have an apple orchard. The government provided the trees about ten years ago, and they have grown well. Just last spring [1989] the government gave us 12,000 yuan for more land changes and asked us to plant more apple trees in the salt land. They provided 15,000 yuan to buy the trees. Many people here disagreed because they feared it would reduce cotton output. I held meetings and kept persuading them, saying that even though the trees would not produce fruit for several years, the income eventually would be greater than for cotton. Most people finally agreed. Unfortunately, many of the apple tree seedlings froze when being shipped from Taian in Shandong Province; also, the masses were not enthusiastic about planting the trees, so many of them died after they were planted. We replanted some, but we will probably not expand our orchards in the future.

We have also planted a lot of tong trees and zao trees (Chinese dates) along the edges of our fields. The tong wood is very valuable. It grows quickly and is water resistant. We use it for coffins. The dates are not as valuable as apples, but they bring 20 yuan a sack. They are planted on the margins of the fields.

Our income has been increased too because we irrigate the fields much more than in the past. All of our fields are irrigated today. Extensive irrigation began in the 1960s. We first used oil-driven pumps to get the water from our wells. We now use electricity. As our allotment of electricity has increased, we have been able to put more water on our fields. We would benefit by using even more, but at least we now do not worry so much about drought, which was very common in the past.

Electricity first came to our village in 1966. The power was so weak it was good for only a few electric lights. Now it is many tens of times stronger and has changed the situation here a lot. The electricity comes from Anyang. We get it from a power-transmitting station in Taiping Village. We were the first village in Six Village Township to have enough power to run an electric flour-grinding mill. The villagers from here and elsewhere all rushed to see it. They were overjoyed that they would no longer have to push heavy grinding stones themselves. We were first because we got special consideration from Taiping Village. Taiping is our neighbor to the north. I had already cultivated a friendly relationship with them, as I had with all of the villages that border the land of our village. In the past there had been a lot of robbery between the villages and a lot of fights. I had taught the villagers here not to fight with Taiping villagers and to help them whenever they ran short of any supplies. Once, I decided to lend them 2,000 yuan when they had economic problems. Later they returned the money. They were grateful, and we have had a good relationship since.

One of the most important changes in the village is in our drinking water. In the past the people drank from shallow wells that carried contagious diseases and had a very high concentration of fluoride. Eighty-five percent of the people and animals here had fluoride bone disease from the drinking water. It bends the bones and gives people curved backs. Some people couldn't straighten their arms and legs by age thirty. It turns teeth brown and eventually makes them fall out. I had lost all of my teeth by age thirty. The ones I have now are false.

In 1980 my uncle Wang Congwu sent the county health organization here to check our water. It had six times the maximum 0.1 part per ton standard for fluoride. We got in touch with the Geology Bureau, and in 1983 they drilled a well 300 meters deep! It cost 70,000 yuan to drill it. The township paid 40,000, the state paid 10,000, and we paid the rest; our contribution was mostly in the form of labor. An electric pump brings up the water from the well. We built a brick water tower and ran pipes to all the houses. All families now have running water in the courtyard. The fluoride level is now 0.05 per ton. It can be drunk without boiling, but we usually boil it anyway. The health of our villagers has been greatly improved since the well was dug. It is probably true that we would not have that well even today had it not been for the influence of my uncle. Many villages in this area with fluoride problems still cannot afford to dig deep wells.

8

Retirement and Retrospective on Leadership

In this chapter Wang Fucheng talks about his principles and the methods he used to govern the village when he was in charge. His narrative reveals why he remained Party secretary for thirty years when the average tenure in that position in surrounding villages was only four years. It also reveals, for better or worse, that he was becoming increasingly out of step with the changing times. He sounds a bit curmudgeonly with his complaints of the way young people dress and act, and his intolerance for gambling and drinking. His own wife regularly gambled in the front courtyard of their house with other neighborhood women, though for very small stakes; and his son, the new Party secretary, downed six or seven bottles of beer when I had lunch with him in a small township eatery. His granddaughters wore bright clothing and sometimes cheap jewelry to school. Clearly, his family did not entirely share his concerns, though from his perspective their behavior might have confirmed his misgivings about current trends. His son, Wang Dejun, disagreed with his father's assertion that fighting had become a serious problem in the village, although he did acknowledge that it had increased in the past several years. Wang Fucheng is undoubtedly right that the increase in the practices he denounces, including some that are clearly illegal—for instance, theft, and the sale of women—is due to the decline of the Communist Party and consequent loosening of social control following the death of Mao, especially after decollectivization. He was more comfortable with greater control, particularly when he exercised it, and is clearly uncomfortable with what he calls "too much freedom." Again, he reveals himself as a man of his time whose time is rapidly passing.

Wang Fucheng:

I retired in 1984, when I was sixty-four. The state was urging older cadres to retire at that time. I thought I was too old, so I talked to the township Party secretary and he agreed to let me retire. I then became a member of the village Party committee and still took care of village problems such as theft, quarreling, fighting, divorces, and so on, until I became ill at the end of 1987.

The township Party secretary insisted that my son, Dejun, succeed me as Party secretary in Houhua Village. I felt it was not proper that my son succeed me. I was afraid that the masses would say we practice a hereditary system in the Party—father and son both Party secretary. The township Party secretary persisted, and finally he made the decision at the township level. Party members in the village then also elected Dejun. Very few people disagreed. I still disagree. In my opinion, Dejun should be the village leader in charge of farm work, not the Party secretary.

As I think back over the course of my thirty years as Party secretary, I think that my most important task has been to maintain unity among the villagers and especially among village cadres. My success in that task is what I'm most proud of. If cadres outside the village don't get along well, they can be transferred. Here in the village we can't do that. Where would we send them? Unity of village cadres is essential for solving problems. We rely on our own cadres; those from the township and county can't settle our problems. Our cadres must have the backing of the masses. How do they win their favor? By doing their jobs well. I tell them not to worry if as many as 10 percent of the people don't back them. There are always thieves, lazy people, and those who care only for their own affairs. The cadres should not fear them. If only 10 percent disagree with you, you may be at ease that you are doing well. There is an old saying, "It is easier to be the head of an army than the head of a village." An army is well disciplined and easy to control, whereas a village has no discipline—there are always troublemakers and many complaints and quarrels. Actually, the troublemakers when I was Party secretary were all poor peasants, those with the best class background. Those who lost land in the land reform were the least trouble because they had been severely suppressed by the government.

From the time we formed our first-level cooperative [1954] until the end of the collective system [1984] there were no problems in this village that I could not handle. That is because I paid close attention to the question of cadre unity. There were seven cadres in each of the six teams, and twelve cadres at the brigade level, fifty-four in all. I kept in close touch with all of them. When there were problems, I would carefully analyze the cause. If a cadre was at fault in a dispute with one of the people, I would talk to him and say he shouldn't beat and curse the masses but should talk to them and

Older women of the village.

get their support, otherwise there would be all kinds of struggles. I would tell him that I would be responsible for all problems.

If two families fought, I would go to both families and investigate to determine right and wrong. I would talk to them and persuade them to calm their anger. If one was a cadre family, I would mainly go there because they should set an example. If the cadre didn't accept my advice, I would go back day after day until he did. Usually after several visits he would say, "Oh, grandfather Fucheng, don't come again. I'll continue to do my work." I would say, "Was it your fault?" He would say, "Yes," and that was the end of it. I almost never criticized a cadre publicly.

Sometimes I would talk to cadres' wives. I'm in an older generation and can do that. I would say they should support their husbands in their work even if the masses cursed them almost to death. They shouldn't urge their husbands to quit. I would explain that in the past we poor people had no land or power or even enough food. Now we are masters. We should hold on to our power. "Your husband is in power. Why shouldn't you be in favor of that?" After several visits to their houses, they would agree with me.

There has been only one cadre I couldn't get along with. He was a vice Party secretary named Wang Baosong. He had a strong personality and a bad temper. He did what he wanted and didn't listen to others. When the big brick kiln was built he wanted to work there and be leader, but he didn't say that directly and I couldn't guess his intention. For some time he simply refused to work as a cadre. I was surprised and went to his house twice. I said if he disagreed with me he could talk with me or with the commune cadres, but he said nothing. I was puzzled for a long time, until we adopted the responsibility system; then he said he would no longer be a cadre. He joined the six families who took over management of the kiln. Today, I still don't know why we didn't get along. Was it his fault? My fault? He didn't come out to greet me when we visited the kiln yesterday. Even during the spring festival he didn't come to visit. "Man's heart is hidden by his skin, a tiger's heart is hidden by his fur."

When handling problems in the village, my policy was to educate people, not punish them. That was the policy of the Party at that time, too, but it was not always followed. I'll give you an example of how I did things. In the western part of the village there was a man named Wang Wenyu. He had a family of five, two of whom were teenage boys who ate a lot. His wife was not a good manager. She was wasteful. As a result, they ran out of grain. Wang Wenyu broke into the brigade storehouse and stole about sixty jin of beans. When the theft was discovered, some people said it should be reported to the police and the culprit should be punished. I said, "No, it must be someone who needs food." Actually, everyone knew who did it. I went to Wang Wenyu's house and told him to confess and to return the beans. In return, I would provide help. I criticized myself in front of him saying I should have known about his problem and given him help earlier. He returned the beans, and the whole family went to the village leaders to ask forgiveness. The leaders all criticized themselves and said to come to them with problems in the future. I reported to the commune that the family had no food. The commune gave them 200 jin of grain. They were very moved and promised to manage their affairs better. Soon they became self-sufficient.

In another case, a man named Zhang Yintang stole thirty coins from production team number three. He was caught and sent to the village headquarters. I saw no point in having him beaten or fined. I said to him, "What you did was your fault, but it was also mine. I did not do a good job of educating you. Let us go together and confess our faults to the whole village. I walked around the village beating a gong, calling everyone together. Zhang Yintang walked behind me carrying a bag with the stolen coins. A large crowd gathered. I criticized myself first. Zhang Yintang was very ashamed. He said he would never steal again, and he hasn't. The whole village was educated by this incident. It was much more effective than beating or fining him. Today the situation is different. Most crimes in the village are no longer handled by the village leaders. The village government is weak and cannot solve big problems. Village leaders often do not want to get involved. The people themselves report crimes to the township police, not to the town leaders. Sometimes it is up to the victim whether a crime will be handled by the village or by the township. Those who are arrested are fined heavily, and often they are severely beaten. There is no longer any ideological education as there was during Chairman Mao's time.

It would not be accurate to say that people were never beaten when I was Party secretary. How we dealt with people depended on the case. About ten years ago, just after the land was redivided, there was a series of thefts in the village. People began to suspect each other. It is a practice in villages when something is stolen for the woman of the household to go out into the street to yell out the family grievance and curse the person they suspect. She does not mention anyone's real name, but it is implied. Things can get very messy. The women play that role because if they are wrong, the man can more easily make up for the mistake. It is more serious if the man falsely accuses someone. The women do the cursing before the case is solved; men do the beating after it is solved. When the thefts began in this village, I knew there would be no peace until we caught the person responsible. We began patrolling the village lanes when people were working out in the fields. Eventually, suspicion fell on a man named Wang Liuxian. He was in his twenties and strong, but very lazy. He never went into the fields to work. We caught him one day when he entered the home of a mute person to search for money. When that person came home unexpectedly, he said he was there to borrow a radio. The mute person did not believe him and reported him to the leaders. We knew immediately that he was the thief. He denied it. I said, "We have a method to make you confess." I took him to the militia office, where they beat him. He immediately admitted that he had stolen from twenty-eight households in the village. I felt strongly that this person deserved the beating. It is very useful in certain cases. It is done in every village. After his confession, a lot of men in the village wanted to beat Wang Liuxian some more. I said, "No, I must turn him over to the police. It is in government hands now." But I could not assuage their anger. Some began to beat him with their bare hands. I yielded, but I did not let them use sticks or other weapons, and I called in the head of the militia to protect him. He was eventually tried and sentenced to one year in prison. He is now out, doing construction work somewhere. He no longer lives in the village.

In some villages there have been problems between families of different surnames. That has not been the case here. Over 80 percent of the village population is in the Wang family, but there are over thirty households with other surnames as well. Five to six are named Du; six to seven, Li; seven to eight, Zhang; three to four, another Wang family; and about ten are in the He lineage. The He family have been in the village longer than anyone else. They were here before the Wangs came from Shanxi Province several hundred years ago. During the thirty years that I was Party secretary there were no quarrels between the different lineages. I didn't treat them differently; I was fair to all. Recently there have been some squabbles between families with different names—society has changed a lot—but none of them have been serious.

The relationship between our village and the surrounding villages is something that I paid a lot of attention to, too. If there are bad relations between neighboring villages, there will be a lot of fights. That won't happen if the cadre's work is done well. I'll give you an example. Someone from Ye Village, which borders us to the northeast, stole a basket of corn and some sweet potatoes from us. The usual practice in the past was for the villagers to beat him black and blue when they caught him, and then fine him. I simply took him to his brigade leader's house, explained the facts, and asked for the corn and sweet potatoes back. That sort of thing happened several times, and I did the same thing each time. The people in Ye Village were moved. Their cadres held a meeting telling the villagers not to steal again. But the cadres there didn't do their work well. There were many contradictions among them. Also, the living standards in Ye Village are lower than here. The stealing continued. For instance, we have apple and pear orchards next to Ye Village land. Students from Ye Village often stole our fruit at harvest time. Once, I caught one of them. I didn't beat him but took him to the school and explained the facts to the teacher. The next day I picked 100 jin of pears and sent them to the school for the students to eat. The teachers were moved and said that Houhua people are generous and good people. We shouldn't steal from them.

Once, when I was on my way to the county seat, I passed a cotton field of our number-four team. I was surprised to see that all of the cotton plants, including the stalks, had been stolen. The team leader and I figured that about eighteen mu of cotton, weighing about 2,000 jin, had been stolen. We figured that it had been done by Ye Village people. I went there to see the cadres. They said, "Fucheng! Why are you here again? Any thefts?" I said, "Two thousand jin of our cotton has been stolen, but I don't think your villagers stole it." The cadres there were clever and knew my intention. They were very worried. They told me to find the cotton, but I didn't look. Then they told the team leaders to search for evidence. They found that about twenty of their people had stolen it. While I was talking, some people came in carrying baskets and confessed to stealing. Soon more came, bringing back the cotton. They brought about 1,000 jin in all to the courtyard of one of the cadres. The cadres said they would make up our loss. I then left. The next day they came to Houhua with 1,000 jin of cotton and 2,000 jin of corn. We in Houhua Village at first refused to accept them, but later we decided to accept the corn and give all the cotton to the thieves. On the following day we returned to Ye Village carrying a number of bottles of wine, as well as meat and vegetable dishes, and had a banquet for the cadres. Some of them were moved to tears. They realized that their villagers had lost face and should be educated. Today we have a very good relationship with them. There is no more stealing.

Although I have been quite successful in solving problems, I have also had some disappointments. The greatest disappointment was the inability to solve the problems between the villagers and the educated youths from Anyang. It was also disappointing to me when some backward people smeared excrement on the door of our gate. That was the year our son, Dejun, got married [1975]. I reported it to the commune cadres. They came and investigated. They wanted to hold a meeting here to find the culprits. I insisted that they not do that. I simply washed the door with water. I wasn't angry. In fact I was glad that those who did it didn't dare reveal their hearts in public. They were either thieves or very lazy people. They weren't class enemies, or I would have been assassinated. They resorted to this sort of thing because they couldn't overthrow me. I did my work well. I thought it useless to investigate a matter of that sort. I didn't mention it any more. Several days later, when the masses saw that I was so calm, they cursed the culprits for me: "You dirty bastards." I then felt more confident.

About a year later, I opened the door and found paper money that is burned for the dead hanging on it. My reactions were the same as they had been in the other incidents. I was not unhappy. I knew that there were advanced and backward masses, that there was class struggle.[1] I have always stood on the side of the masses, serving them, so I have nothing to fear.

I was Party secretary for several decades and worked without stopping for even one day. My only ambition has been to be a good village-level cadre. Throughout my life I have not smoked, drunk alcohol, or stolen anything from the brigade. I have taken no bribes. My life is simple. I don't like wearing new clothes. People describe me as honest, loyal, and reliable. In the time that I was Party secretary in this village, the Party secretary in the township changed nineteen times! I must tell you that one reason I have been able to work well is that my wife has always firmly supported me. She is also a Party member. Without her help, I would have met many more difficulties.

Toward the end of my career as Party secretary I was honored by being elected delegate to the district People's Representative Assembly in Anyang. A district encompasses many counties. I was an agricultural representative for Neihuang County. People in the village elected me, but township officials had decided which villages would send representatives. As I recall, there were five or six delegates chosen from among the twenty-two villages in our township. I had already been a representative for the township of the Neihuang County People's Representative Assembly several times.

My duty as a delegate was to express my opinions and those of the masses. I made speeches several times. We were also given envelopes to express our opinions in writing when the assembly was not in session. There is a special office for receiving the masses' opinions. I am illiterate, so I couldn't write, but three times I had people write for me.

If I had not become ill and were still a delegate today, I know what I would talk about. I would ask why policy has changed. Why are there so many thieves now, and why doesn't the government care? Why is there so much fighting in the villages? Selling women and little girls is more and more common. Even in the old society [before 1949] the law didn't allow that. Why is it recurring?

Right here in this village, four young girls from Sichuan Province have been sold in the past few years. Individual families have bought them as wives. There is no formal wedding ceremony. The girls just live with a young man and are considered married. Mostly they come from very poor families. Some unscrupulous people make their living by selling girls. They convince the girls to come with them, or they kidnap the girls, and then they sell them for 1,000–2,000 yuan. That sort of thing should stop, but there is nothing we can do about it now.

The whole countryside is somehow out of control. People are more likely to beat and curse each other than before, especially the young. If there are several sons in a family, the family is considered powerful. If there is fighting, they will take advantage of it: For instance, several days ago a man in this village was badly beaten and had to be sent to the township clinic. He was beaten because there was a dispute over boundary lines. His family was at a disadvantage because it lacked male power. When I was Party secretary there was much less fighting than now.

Fighting in this village began to increase following the Party's policy of "taking the hats off" class enemies. That meant that we could not control people by calling them class enemies. Also, before the "hats" were removed, the children of former landlords and rich peasants inherited the class label of their parents. To avoid criticism, they worked hard and were even more obedient than the children of poor and lower-middle peasants. But since class labels have been removed, they have engaged in more quarreling and fighting because they had been silent for so long. Now that there is no more class struggle, it is harder to maintain control.

Drunkenness and gambling are beginning to be serious problems here too. From the leaders to the common people there is a lot of drinking. Alcohol is sold everywhere. All four small shops in this village sell it. There are big factories for manufacturing alcohol in both Neihuang town and Anyang. When people want to solve problems, they often drink together first and then discuss the issues. Sometimes that makes things worse. Alcohol affects production in this village and elsewhere. People drink when guests come. There is no fixed time for drinking; it is done any time of the day. People get drunk and then rest for a whole day. Then they sometimes quarrel with their families. It is mostly young men who do this. Women drink very little.

Some women do gamble. People play *paijiu* and mahjong. They also waste money by eating a lot when they gamble at each other's houses. Many do it just for recreation and don't use much money, but some bet a lot and then make trouble. Many lose, few win. Young men who lose curse and beat people. There is theft and instability. That is the most dangerous thing in the village now. The masses are not satisfied with the situation, but no one can control it.

Young people have begun to pursue freedom now. If people have too much freedom, they are likely to be uncontrollable. Young men, aged fifteen to thirty, have all changed. They wear strange clothes, red and green, the brighter and more colorful the better. They let their hair grow long and go to barber shops to have it shaped and curled. You can't tell if they are male or female. Some carry knives under their clothes. The masses say that policies should be enforced, that there should be more education, that more criminals should be sent to the courts, and that those who deserve execution should be executed.

Some people say that problems in the village are related to our increased prosperity. Income is higher than in the past and can be used either for production or for activities like gambling. In a village there is a lot of spare time, especially after harvest and planting seasons. Our work is seasonal. It is not like that in a factory, where all have regular jobs to do. There is indeed unemployment, or underemployment, if you want to call it that, that provides opportunities for doing bad deeds. But so-called unemployment should be seen in this way: If you say you have nothing to do, it is because you don't want to do anything. There is always work to do. For instance, if you tend your cotton well, you can get 200 jin per mu. Some lazy people get only 50–60 jin. The land quality is the same. The difference is in human energy and will.

It is only in the past three or four years [since 1984] that the situation in the village has been deteriorating. The village is still better off than some around it, but not as much as in the past, because the leaders now are all young and lack experience. Furthermore, they no longer have authority. Since decollectivization and the break up of the brigade, the Party secretary is not really in charge. The Communist Party has lost its power. We seldom have meetings of Party members now. Many Party members don't even pay their dues. That is the case in other villages, too. The whole county is in disorder.

The commune system had its good points. Society was more stable; there was less theft. We won't go back to it, though, because we wouldn't develop economically if we did. But under the collective system we educated people to do good deeds, to help people, not to beat and smash and rob. I would like to educate young people in this village today by asking them to remember past hardships, to remember when we had to go out begging, when people went for days without eating. We couldn't imagine how fortunate we would become. We mustn't forget that only under Chairman Mao's leadership could we have the prosperous life we have today.

You asked me about the Lei Feng campaign before.[2] I didn't pay much attention to it in the past, but I have learned more about Lei Feng since you mentioned him last year. He spent his life serving the people. He served them heart and soul. He died for the people, fearing neither hardship nor death. He is a good example for all youth around the country. In the past, people knew how to learn from Lei Feng. Now they don't. Lei Feng was a good cadre. Today there are some good cadres and some bad. Some are corrupt and take bribes. They use public funds to influence people. They won't solve the masses' problems if they are not given gifts. That sort of thing has had a bad influence on the masses, especially on young people. We need a new policy dealing with daily life in the villages.

9

Houhua Village Under New Leadership, 1984–1990

The principal narrator in this chapter is Wang Fucheng's son, Wang Dejun. The interviews were conducted in April 1990. Dejun had succeeded his father as Party secretary, but it is clear that he had little enthusiasm for the job. His attitudes are a good illustration of the general malaise that had overtaken the Communist Party in the 1980s. I wanted to learn from the new Party secretary about recent changes in the village and future prospects. Our discussion covered a range of topics including politics, clan matters, women, birth control, divorce, health, education, and religion. He was most animated when we discussed religion. Indeed, that topic was the focus of village attention and conversation when I visited in 1990. A new temple to a village deity was in the final stages of completion, and a new clan temple was being constructed. Traditional funeral rites had been fully restored after having been forbidden by the Communists for several decades. I was privileged to observe a funeral while I was there. A matron of the He clan had just died, and a great many relatives had gathered to pay their respects. When I asked if I could photograph the ceremonies, the He family enthusiastically agreed, for there was not another camera in the village and they were delighted to have a photographic record.

The most significant aspect of the proceedings for me was the choice of burial site. After the family had paraded through the village in their white sack-cloth mourning clothes, accompanied by musicians playing wind instruments and drums, they headed out of town into fields sown with winter wheat, and there, in the middle of their best crop land, they had dug a hole for the coffin. In traditional fashion, they had consulted a "wind and water expert" (a geomancer) to find the most auspicious final resting place. It did not matter to the wind and water expert that the field was not really theirs, that it belonged to the village and was supposed to be included in a general land redistribution every ten years. It seemed clear to me that there would be no further land redistribution, that the land allotments were already considered private. They could not be sold, but neither could they be taken away from a family whose ancestors resided there. When I asked Wang Dejun about that, he responded: "We will face that problem when we come to it." Later, when I visited in 1994, Wang Dejun showed me an ordinance that had just been issued by the central government that confirmed my supposition. It stated that land would not be redistributed again for at least thirty years. It was clear that the responsibility system that had come into effect a decade earlier had been significantly altered.

Shamans are playing a role in village life again after having been denounced as charlatans by the Communists and forbidden to practice. I met a shaman who had come to Houhua Village to call the spirit of a Wang family ancestor to enter a temple newly constructed in his honor. She was standing at the door of the temple, having just come out of a trance. Her eyes were bloodshot, and she was having trouble adjusting to the light. When she spotted me, she smiled, came over and held my hand, and said, "We have been expecting you for a long time." Unnerved, I acted as ordinary as possible. We parted after exchanging pleasantries. I still do not know what she meant—whether she thought that I was the returned spirit of the expected ancestor, or if she was just being polite to a foreigner.

The temple-building phenomenon was apparent in numerous villages in the area. Zhonghua, the village abutting Houhua to the south, had just had a temple to the Mother God built when I visited in 1990 and had hired an opera troupe to inaugurate it. Several thousand people were in attendance at the opera when I arrived. When the attention of the audience shifted from the singers to the spectacle of an unexpected foreigner, I left. That incident was symbolic: For all the excitement about the return of traditional religion and the continuing popularity of traditional opera, there was also a growing awareness of, and interest in, what is new and foreign. With virtually all of the village children now attending school, where they study science and foreign languages; with the purchase of television sets by almost half of the households in the village; and with changes in the economy that are beginning to bring even the most backward villages into the world market, the impetus for a return to traditional beliefs and practices will undoubtedly be modified and, ultimately, superceded by the global imperatives of contemporary institutions and practices.

The New Party Secretary Wang Dejun

Wang Dejun:

I became Party secretary in 1984 when my father retired. Today the role of the Party secretary is not nearly as important as before. The large building in the center of the village that used to be the site of meetings of all the brigade members is no longer used and is falling apart. There are holes in the roof, and the windows are broken. Two cotton-processing machines are now kept in it. Our plan is to repair it and then sell it for living quarters.

Actually, even speaking as head of the Party in this village, I'm happy to see the power of the Party reduced. I don't even want to be a cadre. I don't care about the 300 yuan I get each year for being Party secretary. I could make much more money if I spent more time taking care of our land, or if I became a peddler or took a second occupation. I'm kept too busy with village business and having to go to meetings in the township all the time to hear about documents issued by the Party central committee. I've talked several times to the township Party secretary about quitting. He won't agree, and neither will the Party members. I keep the position because I feel it is my responsibility. I joined the Party in 1984. That is not long ago. I feel an emotional obligation to the Party.

There is some dissatisfaction with the Party now. Some Party members don't pay dues and have no interest in Party affairs. This will change because we will educate them. Right now, there is some study of central committee documents by Party members, but very little.

There are currently 34 Party members in the village in a population of about 1,400; 1,000 villagers are old enough to be Party members. A lot of the Party members are quite old. Six of them are women. All of the women joined the Party before liberation or in the 1950s. Some young women joined during the Cultural Revolution in the late 1960s, but they have married and left the village. No women have joined since then because it is felt that problems here are suitable for men to settle and not for women. They should pay more attention to household affairs. Some women apply to join the Party now, but the Party members must check their qualifications and observe them; they have found that the women are not mature enough and cannot fulfill the tasks assigned them. Sometimes women are not very active in public affairs. To join the Party you must have the people's confidence. They must be able to rely on you. Party members are supposed to be models for political activities when they occur.

The main task of the Party branch right now is birth control. We ask women to participate in publicizing birth control information. And there is a woman director of women's issues in the village. Population planning has been an important Party task in the village since 1977, but for a few years we neglected it. For the past two years it has become the main Party task again. The population of Houhua has grown from about 800 in 1949 to 1,420 now, and the amount of cultivated land and land per person has steadily dropped. In 1971 there were 3,160 cultivated mu; now there are 2,472. That is why population control is so important now. The people know it affects their livelihood.

Some time ago if a couple signed an agreement to have only one child, the brigade gave them 5 yuan a month. That policy lasted only two years, 1974–1976. Most people after that continued to have at least two children. Then we had a policy of fining people 630 yuan after the second child and having either the man or the woman have an operation so they wouldn't have more children. If there was a third child, the fine would be 1,370 yuan. Some preferred to pay the fine rather than have an abortion. And actually we did not enforce the policy very strictly for several years. Today there is no choice whether to pay a fine or have an abortion. We make them have an abortion. There is a birth control clinic in the county seat where they are sent.

The village does not give birth control devices except IUDs for women. Unfortunately they can cause pain in the back and legs and also infection. There is nothing we can do about it.

The other main task of the Party secretary now is to settle disputes. There are not many disputes here that have to be settled by cadres—maybe ten to twenty a year. There are few thefts, two or three a year, sometimes none. If we catch a thief, we hold a meeting. If there is proof, and if the theft is not large, the people involved settle the issue themselves. Otherwise, we go to the township government.

Some quarrels are settled by clan elders. There is no one head of the Wang clan in our village, but for every thirty to fifty households there are older people who enjoy a particular respect. They are called on to officiate at ceremonies for births, deaths, and marriages. When important guests come, the elder sits in the principal seat in the north, facing south. Often people discuss their problems with them, and the issues are settled under their charge. There is no conflict between family heads and the Party here. The Party is in charge. I don't consult family elders when I make decisions as Party secretary. But people do respect the older generation. For instance, it is a custom here to put the name of your father on your roof beam when you build a new house, even though you own it. Our house was built two years ago. You can see the name of my father, Wang Fucheng, on the ceiling.

Occasionally there are disputes that cannot be settled by one village alone. I sometimes have to meet with the heads of other villages. For instance, last July someone from Ye Village was raising sheep in land that belonged to our village. One of our villagers caught six or seven sheep and brought them here. Cadres from Ye Village came and asked for the sheep, and we had a long discussion. Finally they agreed to pay thirty yuan and not raise sheep on our land again. We then gave back the sheep. That sort of thing happens two or three times a year.

Another example is when a quarrel between a wife and husband extends to her family in another village. If the couple wants a divorce, cadres from both villages discuss the issues and try to get them to continue to live together. If the village cadres can't convince them, we report it to the township Judicial Affairs Bureau, and if they don't succeed they give the case to the county authorities. There are not many divorces, but still there are some. There was one here last year, and this year there is another couple who want a divorce.

The township and county still send people here to inspect the village and deal with problems. One person in the township has special responsibility for this village. If we have a problem we cannot settle, we first report it to him, and he reports it to other leaders. I'll give you an example of such a problem. Last spring we wanted to adjust the property lines for houses in the [former] fifth production team. Many people were dissatisfied and wanted more space. This is a big problem as population grows. People are not supposed to expand their houses and courtyards onto farm land. We have already lost quite a lot of farm land. We couldn't solve that problem and neither could the township, so it has been given to the county Land Bureau. It is not settled yet.

The issue of residential property lines causes many arguments. Just this week someone from a nearby village was murdered. He had his head cut off because he placed his bricks across his neighbor's line. There is a custom in this village of digging four holes, three to four feet deep, and pouring lime in them to show the corners of the courtyard. This is used as proof if there are quarrels later. We usually lay bricks several inches inside the line when we build a house so that water won't pour off the roof into the neighbor's courtyard. There is a case here right now where a new house has been built that sheds rainwater into the neighbor's courtyard. The two families fought, and all of the males on both sides were so badly injured they had to go to medical clinics. One family went to a clinic in Liucun Township, the other to one in Jingdian. Some were there for several days. I couldn't settle the issue, so I wrote a letter to the township Judicial Affairs Bureau. They have now asked the owners of the new house to shorten their roof.

Wang Fucheng:
   The problem of more houses and less land is very serious. Today when young people get married they want a new house. When a new wife comes to the village, no matter how many things she asks her husband's family to buy, they will agree because now they have some extra money. So, they

want not only a new house but a large one for all their things. In the past, the total space allotted for each household courtyard was 0.35 mu. Now it is 0.45 mu, but that still doesn't satisfy people. Some are even building on the agricultural responsibility land assigned to them. They regard it as their own even though that land is owned by the whole village and will be readjusted every ten years. I don't know how we'll solve that problem in the future. We don't have a plan for future building.

Wang Dejun continues:

Almost everyone in the village has built a new house in the past several years. The cost of building is going up. Two years ago when we built this house, bricks cost 30 yuan per thousand [about US$6 at the time]. Now they cost 80 yuan. That is because coal for firing the bricks is so much more expensive. It now costs 1 yuan for 12 jin of coal. That is much more than before. I don't remember the exact amount. New houses are built by a crew of young men who specialize in house building when they are not farming. A house can be built in several days. The owner gives the workers food and cigarettes and pays them a wage. It costs about 2,000 yuan [US$400] to build a medium-size brick house with three rooms and kitchen and storage rooms outside in the courtyard.

The village is much more prosperous than it used to be. The household responsibility system is far better than the collective system we had before. The average income per working person is 1,200 yuan per year after tax. The top household in the village has seven working members and earned an average of 1,500 yuan each, or 10,500 yuan total, last year. Except for the four Five Guarantees Households, the poorest household earned a total of 1,000 yuan. It had only two people in it. They couldn't make it through the year and had to borrow from relatives and friends. The loans are made without interest. Some people borrow from a bank—especially if they need money to build a new house. The bank charges 1.5 percent per month, or 18 percent per year.

The standard of living is a bit higher here than in some of the surrounding villages because we have more land than many of them and we have more electrical power. The amount and the cost of electrical power depends on the source. Ours comes from Anyang and is cheaper than electricity in, for instance, Qiankou Village, which is only a few li from here but gets its power from another source. Also, the transmitting station is in Taiping Village on our northern border. We have good relations with them, and they take good care of us. We could use more electrical power. Electricity has a great effect on agricultural production. We irrigate all of our fields using electrical pumps. We would like to irrigate more. That would raise our production.

Even with more electricity, though, it is going to be difficult to raise production very much. We already irrigate all of our fields, we use the newest hybrid seeds, and we use as much fertilizer as our fields will currently take. How will we raise our standard of living from now on? We have thought of raising more pigs, goats, and chickens. We have also thought of building a processing plant for cotton or alcohol, or building a paper-making factory, but we can't afford it. There are no bank loans for such things now. It will be difficult to raise our standard of living.

The health of the villagers has improved a lot in the past several years. The infant mortality rate is very low now, and life expectancy is over seventy. Women live longer than men, but only by about two years. Almost all of the men smoke cigarettes. We know it is supposed to be harmful, but frankly we don't see that. There is some cancer, but those who don't smoke get it, too. Some older men have bronchial disease, but not many. A much greater medical problem here is stroke. I don't know the cause.

The schools here could be improved a lot. More education would help our production. People could learn more about cotton and corn from books. The courses in the school and all of the textbooks are determined by the central government. Here we have a five-year elementary school system. In cities and more advanced areas it is six years. We will convert to six years in 1991. One hundred percent of the school-age children in this village enter elementary school. About 7 to 8 percent leave before graduating. There are four junior secondary schools [grades 6–8] in Liucun Township, and a senior secondary school [grades 9–11] in Neihuang county seat. Eighty percent of our elementary school graduates go to junior secondary school, but only about 10 percent of them go on to senior secondary school. They ride bikes or walk the six li to the township school, but they would have to board at the county school. Very few students go on to higher education. Two years ago, one student went to Qinghua University in Beijing. Recently, one went to Jiaotong University in Shanghai and one to Zhengzhou University in our province. Another one went to a normal college. I'm not very satisfied with my children's education because the level of education in the schools is too low. Also, the children must help with farming in the busy season and don't spend enough time in school.

We don't want our son, Yanwei, to go beyond junior secondary school. Besides, he plays all the time and doesn't have much interest in school work. Among our three children, our youngest daughter, Yongxia, does best in school. She is always reading and is the cleverest of the three. If she does well in the entrance examinations, we will urge her to go as far as she can.

We have had some adult education in the village. We built a small building for a library and spent several hundred yuan for books, but the villagers

A small shrine to a god.

don't go there often. There is no teacher to help them study. We do have an agricultural technician who comes in from the county to pass along farming information. He is a junior secondary school graduate and did additional study in the county for some time. The village collects money to pay him.

Return to Traditional Beliefs and Practices

Many village temples and shrines were destroyed before liberation, but there were still some large temples in the village until the Cultural Revolution. All were demolished in the campaign to destroy the "Four Olds." Now some are being rebuilt, but most of the shrines are only about one meter high. There are a lot of them in the village. People burn incense there to the Grandmother God, the Grandfather God, the Goddess of Mercy, the God of Wealth, and the Great Jade Emperor. By far the most important temple in this village now was built just this year [1990]. Wang Changbin, a former village school teacher, can tell you about it.

Auspicious Grandfather Temple (1990).

Wang Changbin:
The new temple has just been built to house the spirit of the Auspicious Grandfather (Lao Jiye). This Auspicious Grandfather was a member of the fourteenth generation of our Wang clan. He was born in this village during the Kang Xi reign [1662–1722] of the Qing Dynasty. Although he became known by the name Hong Keni, his real name was Wang Jinlu. It is recorded in our family record book. For reasons no longer known, he was murdered in Wangu Village in Hua County. After that event the people in Wangu knew no peace until, eventually, they built a temple and a statue to placate Hong Keni. Tranquility returned, and Hong Keni became known as the Auspicious Grandfather of Wangu (Wangu Lao Jiye).

Wang Dejun:
There are a number of folktales about Hong Keni. I'll tell you another one. This guy, who is now known as Auspicious Grandfather, was a village bully. He was lazy and did no field work. Whenever a family had a good meal, he would barge in and eat with them. Eventually he began killing pigs, chickens, and goats in the village and forcing the owner to cook them for him. Finally the villagers decided to kill him. He found out and fled to

Wangu in Hua County. There he continued to be a bully until some people of that village strangled him during an opera performance. Shortly thereafter, a child of one of the stranglers fell ill. A spirit medium said it was Hong Keni taking revenge. So they kowtowed to Hong Keni's spirit and burned incense and the child recovered. Later, another child got sick and they did the same thing. That child also recovered, so they decided to build a temple. The temple, when it was built, contained a statue of Hong Keni. One day, two sisters entered the temple. One of them looked at the statue and exclaimed how handsome he looked. She died soon after she returned home, so the people of Wangu married her to the god, thinking that he had claimed her for a wife.

Wang Changbin:
There is another story concerning that name, which reinforces the story that Hong Keni loved to eat. *Ji*, the written character for "auspicious" in Auspicious Grandfather, has the same sound as *ji*, the written character for "chicken." Some say that Hong Keni was so fond of chicken that he was known originally as the Chicken Grandfather. Whatever the case may be, we now use the *ji* character meaning auspicious.

The Auspicious Grandfather Temple was very sacred to the people in Wangu for about two hundred years, but here in Houhua it was just a topic of idle discussion. During the Cultural Revolution when Chairman Mao said to destroy all the old temples and wipe out superstition, no one dared even discuss these matters. But recently people have been telling stories about the Auspicious Grandfather. The more they talk, the more sacred he becomes. They say he can cure disease and prevent disaster. In the past few years, several people have become ill here—Wang Fucheng, the vice Party secretary, and I have all had serious health problems. Some people thought that such problems might have been prevented if they believed in gods, lit incense, and kowtowed. They also said that our ancestor, the Auspicious Grandfather, wanted to return to his old home. Several clan meetings were held, and Wang Xianliu was elected to be in charge of collecting money and building a Green Dragon Treasure Pavilion for our Auspicious Grandfather.

To prepare for this, a famous "incense child" [*xiang tong*, a spirit medium] named Little Dun Zenglan was invited to come from Double Tranquility Township to "open the palace" by speaking sacred words. Many people gathered at the proposed temple site, and several hundred fell to their knees and performed the kowtow. The incense child sat down, closed her eyes, opened her mouth, and stretched out her hands. She yawned several times and then began moaning and groaning. Her voice got louder and louder. She said, though maybe these are not the exact words:

Recently added temple entrance (1994).

Incense from the burner brightens the air
Three feet above it a god is there
The good families all listen for you
Auspicious Grandfather, they are opening a palace for you
Auspicious Grandfather of Wangu, reveal your soul
Auspicious Grandfather, they truly desire your homecoming
They will build a proper Green Dragon Treasure Pavilion
It is not right that you left the good families
Auspicious Grandfather, return home and fill the air with laughter
The whole village of Houhua is making preparations
Auspicious Grandfather, when you return to Hua Village
There will be peace for 100 li around
Auspicious Grandfather, return home, they will build a treasure pavilion
It is their true desire to sculpt a statue and sing operas
The good families are all arousing the people
They are shaking their purses to make contributions
"If you give but a cent, it will not be considered too little
If you give a yuan, you will be remembered clearly."

Wang Changbin, retired schoolteacher (1989).

She repeated the final two lines, the appeal for money, many times. About 90 percent of the Wang families donated from ten to forty yuan each. People from other villages donated, too. Wang Fucheng and I donated even though we don't believe in gods. Probably over 80 percent of the old people here believe, and at least half of the others at least half believe. Even the doctors in this village contributed money, and if they hadn't, their families would have. Some doctors from the county hospital whose parents were ill also contributed.

Wang Fucheng:
My wife went there to ask the god to protect Wang Fucheng and cure his illness. She said: "Wang Fucheng is now giving you ten yuan."

Li Suzhen, Wang Dejun's wife:
This temple has become one of the best known in the area for curing disease. I strongly believe in the power of the god. Ninety percent of the women in this village believe in the god, and about 50 percent of the men do. I do not know why more women than men believe. I'll give you an ex-

ample of the god's power. Zhang Changsun's wife had a bladder disease. After she promised money to the god, the disease was cured. She also took medicine, but the god cured her, not the medicine.

Wang Dejun:
Nonsense. Superstition.

Li Suzhen:
When you were having so much trouble sleeping, I secretly went to the god and you were cured.

Wang Dejun:
I don't believe any of it. But it is true that a lot of people do. People have come from as far as Beijing to worship in our temple. This village now has its own incense child who supposedly interprets the words of the god.

Li Suzhen:
The god chose her himself. She is learning gradually.

Wang Dejun:
Much of the money for the temple was raised by having an opera performance. From the twelfth to the sixteenth day of the lunar calendar, there was a major opera performance in the village sung by the Hua County Henan Opera Troupe. It cost us 3,000 yuan a day, but we made 7,000–8,000 yuan each day in addition. Hundreds of people from nearby villages came. We raised quite a bit more than the cost of building the temple. The money is handled by a temple management committee of five or six people headed by the village electrician, Wang Xianliu. Extra funds will be used for temple expansion and repair and for other religious purposes only. Anything left over will be put in the bank.

Li Suzhen:
If the money were misused, the god would be angry and cause disease.

Wang Dejun:
The temple cost less to build than an ordinary house of the same size because all of the labor was voluntary. I also helped by passing bricks. We began building the temple on the second day of the second month in 1990. It is completed now, including the paintings of saints inside and three god statues in the front. They were sculpted by Wei Fengqiao, a seventy-seven-year-old man who was formerly in a theatrical troupe in Neihuang. He is very talented. He goes from place to place now, sculpting statues.

Wang Fucheng:

Actually, some of the money left over from building the Auspicious Grandfather Temple is being used to rebuild the Wang Family Temple (Wang Jia Miao). That money was all donated by Wang family members, not by others. We have also asked all the Wang families to donate ten yuan each. The old Wang family temple was torn down on the twentieth day of the 1990 new year. The new one is now almost completed. Yellow and green roof tiles have just arrived from Hua County. They are hard to get and very expensive. The whole temple will cost over 10,000 yuan. When completed, it will have a three-section main hall, a courtyard, and a gate with a small room on either side to house Wang family members visiting from other places.

As you know, the Communist Party does not believe in gods, so it doesn't approve of the Auspicious Grandfather Temple, but it doesn't interfere because the Party branch is too weak to do anything about it. When Chairman Mao was in control, that was not the case. The Party doesn't object to the family temple, however. Its purpose is to remember our ancestors, and that is not regarded as superstition. Even during the Cultural Revolution the family temple was not destroyed. The Wang family all agreed not to destroy it.

Wang Dejun:

We now have big funeral ceremonies again. We don't consider them superstition, either. When people in the village die, all are buried. None is cremated as the Party advocates. There is a public graveyard in the salt area that was established in the 1970s. Everyone is supposed to be buried there, but people prefer to bury their dead in their own farm fields. As Party secretary, I do not try to change that because it is popular in the whole district. In fact, I too will bury our family dead in the fields.

The funeral ceremony is basically the same for all. When someone dies, the younger generation put on white clothing and visit all the relatives in the village. They kowtow and ask them to come to their house to discuss funeral arrangements. They decide together who should play musical instruments, who should go to other villages to inform relatives, and who should cook for the guests.

The corpse is ordinarily buried on the fifth day after death. On the third day guests from other places come to the village. Each brings a piece of white cloth showing that they are a relative. Then the younger generation has a procession in the streets: They carry sticks with white paper coiled around them and walk to the Earth Temple, where they and the close relatives kowtow to the Earth God. There are two Earth Temples, one in the east of the village and one in the west. This whole process is known as "pressing paper" (*ya zhi*)—I don't know why. At noon, the man in charge

He family funeral procession (1990).

of the funeral announces that the burial will be on the fifth day and all relatives should come.

On the fourth day the sacrifices begin. The married daughters and granddaughters come first and offer food, placing it on a table before the coffin. They offer 100 steamed buns, 100 jin of meat, 20 bottles of liquor, 10 cartons of cigarettes, and 200 to 500 yuan. The in-law families also come and bring food. The amount depends on how well-to-do they are. Ten of those families make large sacrifices. When they leave, they take half of the sacrifice with them and then bring it back the next day. During this process on the fourth day, thirteen or fourteen people play various musical instruments in front of the gate of the deceased, and two sit in front of the coffin, playing. The younger generation kowtow continuously, one hundred times or more, in front of the coffin. Then they go into the street, blowing instruments and singing operas. This lasts until one or two o'clock in the morning.

On the fifth day, the younger generation go out to meet the guests. When all arrive, they eat a banquet made from the food that was sacrificed. The eldest son then breaks a bowl on the ground that had been used for burning paper money for the dead. I don't know why he breaks the bowl, but it has been a custom for as long as anyone can remember. There follows a parade to the burial ground, with twenty-four people carrying the coffin through

Burying the deceased matriarch in the middle of the family's best field (1990).

Wang Dejun standing next to tablets inscribed with names of village households that contributed to the construction of the new Wang Family Temple (1994).

the streets. The coffin bearers have cloths in their mouths soaked with alcohol to mask the smell of the corpse. Relatives and others carry rings of flowers and paper statues. At the burial ground, a hole has been dug. The direction of the hole has been determined by a Yin-Yang master. The coffin is placed in the hole, and a large pile of paper money is burned. The wife of the oldest son throws a handful of soil on each of the four corners of the coffin. That begins the burial. It is completed with spades used by the twenty-four people who carried the coffin.

Twenty-eight days after the death, the relatives come again to offer sacrifices. One year and then three years later they do the same thing. They burn paper money and bring steamed buns, eggs, meat, and liquor. After the last ceremony they sometimes invite opera troupes to perform. That completes the ceremonies.

Some people believe that the spirits of the dead continue to exist, so they go on with activities for the dead. I say that spirits of the dead just vanish. But we do record the names of the dead on huge cloths. There are five of them now that contain the Wang family tree showing the generations. Until the Cultural Revolution, they were hung in the ancestral temple for fifteen days during the New Year holiday. They will be hung there again when the new temple is completed. Except at New Year, the cloths and the Wang *Family Register* are kept, in rotation, by the family elders.

Wang Fucheng:

The Wang *Family Register* now records the names of eighteen generations of the descendants of Wang Erlao, our founding ancestor. Wang Erlao came to this area from Hongtong County in Shanxi Province several hundred years ago. There are six large branches of Wang Erlao's descendants now, with 4,000-some households. Many live outside Houhua Village. There are Wangs of our line in Puyang and in Hua County, and even in Shandong Province. Each large branch pays respect to its own founding ancestor, but we all worship Wang Erlao. On the first day of the new year after our new temple is completed, Wang family members from many places will come back here to kowtow and burn incense.

10

Facing an Uncertain Future: Houhua Village, 1994

When I left Wang Fucheng after interviewing him in 1989, he said the following as we parted:

Two years ago, about a month after you were here the first time, I was awakened early in the morning by someone from the commune [township] who asked me to come with him right away. I immediately got up, washed, brushed my teeth, dressed, and went with him. We arrived at the township office at about 7:30 A.M. The commune secretary invited me to breakfast and then asked me to go to Zhengzhou (the capital city of Henan Province). He said I was too old to take the bus over the rough roads to Neihuang county seat, and that I should go in a three-wheeled motorcycle. He and the township leader went by bus. Once we got on the paved road at Jiang Village, the motorcycle driver went much too fast. We covered the thirty li in no time. When we stopped in Neihuang, I couldn't move or talk. I could make sounds, but they had no meaning. I soon passed out and was carried to the hospital. I was there for four days and then in another place in Neihuang for three months. I missed my home, so I came back here. My right side is still mostly paralyzed. I don't have much hope for my future.

I want to tell you about a village custom. When you are in the village, you are more likely to be accepted if you call people by family terms. You should call me *da ge* (older brother). I'll call you *xiong di* (younger brother). My son will call you *shu* (uncle), and his children will call you *ye ye* (grandfather). You call them *sun zi* (grandchild). Call my wife *sao zi* (elder brother's wife). It is a village custom that you can tell any joke to a *sao zi*. You can make any kind of fun and it will be no problem.

Wang Xianghua and Wang Fucheng after his stroke (1989).

You know, I have told you all these things about my life because I like you. I wouldn't talk this way to the township cadres, not for 10,000 yuan. Sometimes I worry because I have spoken so openly.

I am a poor man and have no gift to give you. I can only give you this notebook that was given to me as a delegate to the district People's Representative Assembly in Anyang. It is not valuable, but it is a gift from the heart.

You should write to us two or three times a year. You can ask questions by mail. My son will read the letters to me. If you still have questions, it will make me feel useful. I hope that you will come back often.

I have returned twice since that departure in 1989—in 1990 and 1994. On the latter occasion, the reception was particularly warm. I had brought members of my family and the Wang family had done everything possible to make us feel welcome. Wang Xianghua (Wang Fucheng's wife) held my wife Cynthia's hand for a long time while they conversed affectionately, in mutually unintelligible languages. Amy and John (my daughter and son-in-law) were the object of intense, friendly scrutiny by Wang Fucheng's three

Wang family and author's family (1994). *Back row, from left*: Yanxia, Yongxia, Li Suzhen, Yanwei, Wang Dejun, John Tomasi. *Front row*: Amy Tomasi, Wang Xianghua, author, Wang Fucheng, Cynthia Seybolt.

teenage grandchildren. We took a lot of photographs and ate a huge and delicious banquet that had been catered from Liucun Township. Typically, the banquet was exclusively for males and for the foreign female guests. The Wang family women, after setting up the tables, ate elsewhere. Presumably they had set aside some of the banquet food for themselves, but it would have been impolite for us to inquire.

It was evident that the township government had helped with the cost of the banquet. There were numerous meat and fish dishes, a rare treat in Houhua Village, where even in this time of relative prosperity, meat is consumed only a few times a year; and there was Maotai, the fabulously expensive 140-proof liquor that is reserved for high officials and foreign guests, when it is available at all. Wang Dejun had received a bottle from his famous great uncle, Wang Congwu, when he had visited him in Beijing. The township Party secretary was there to enjoy the meal with us. He had dropped the air of formality and of faintly concealed suspicion that had been evident in previous encounters. I was now an old friend.

Author's wife, Cynthia, with Wang Xianghua (1994).

Li Suzhen, Wang Yongxia, and Wang Yanxia (1994).

In subsequent days, after my family had departed for the United States via Shanghai, I returned to Houhua Village to resume the discussions with Wang Fucheng and Wang Dejun that we had begun seven years earlier. It was July and very hot, nearly 100 degrees Fahrenheit. We sat in the shade of the hawthorn tree in Wang Fucheng's courtyard and ate locally grown watermelons, a specialty of the region, as we talked. As I looked around the village, there were numerous signs of increasing prosperity. Many more households had decorated their courtyard gates with expensive painted and glazed tiles depicting traditional heroes and gods, auspicious animals, and other symbols of good luck. The village temple dedicated to Lao Ji Ye had almost doubled in size with the addition of an outer room for praying and burning incense. And most surprising of all was the addition of a bathing room attached to one of the outer buildings in Wang Dejun's courtyard. It had a deep tile tub with an electric heating unit for use in winter, the first such contrivance in the village. Wang Dejun also had a refrigerator, another extravagance that I had seen nowhere else in Houhua or in any of the surrounding villages. Wang Fucheng's house did not have these luxuries, nor would Wang Fucheng have been interested in having them. Father and son represented different eras and had different interests and aspirations. I did not ask Wang Dejun how he could afford the new amenities in his house. I suspect that they are either manifestations of the generosity of his great uncle or of the perquisites of holding the highest office in the village—or both. He had told me that the family income from farming was just about at the median level for the village.

Having observed numerous signs of prosperity, I was surprised to learn that income in the village had fallen in the past two years and that both father and son were pessimistic about the future. The cotton crop had failed twice due to disease, and no remedy was in sight. The two Wangs blamed the government for problems that currently beset the village, saying that the urban bureaucrats were neglecting and even exploiting agriculture. They saw little hope for significant improvement in the future, barring a change in government policy. Wang Fucheng was forthright in placing responsibility squarely on the shoulders of Deng Xiaoping, Mao Zedong's successor. Deng had created a new order characterized by increased prosperity on the one hand, and political and economic insecurity, official corruption, and material inequality on the other. I was not surprised to hear Wang Fucheng express nostalgia for the past and reiterate his admiration for Mao Zedong. At a time that much of the world was taking an increasingly negative view of the Chairman,[1] he was still a hero for Wang Fucheng.

Wang Dejun was more circumspect than his father when talking about both Mao and Deng, and he was not quite as pessimistic, though he too saw little hope for the future without a change in government policy. What he and other villagers wanted from the government was higher prices for their crops from the state purchasing monopoly, lower prices for manufactured goods such as fertilizer and for services such as electricity, lower taxes, easier credit, and a crackdown on corruption. Those are aspirations that the rural populace in general had had for years, but it was clear from numerous remarks during our discussions that there was growing resentment of government policies because they were thought to favor urban over rural areas. If the Wangs are at all representative, the peasantry in China in 1994 could not be counted on to support the current government in a crisis.

Wang Fucheng:
Since you were here four years ago, life is better in some respects and worse in others. You will notice that people are wearing better clothing, especially young people. They are paying more attention to fashion. Even some of the older people have new clothing. Many people have also spent money decorating their houses and gates with expensive glazed tiles. But actually, these things are deceiving. The income of the village was stagnant for two years after you left and then dropped sharply in the next two years, from an average of 1,200 yuan per person per year to 700 yuan.[2] That is gross income, before taxes. People still have some money to spend on things like clothes and tiles because formerly they used whatever they could save to build new houses. The houses are built now, and people can spend on other things. But there isn't much money. Both taxes and prices have increased while our income has decreased.

Wang Dejun:
The main reason for the drop in income is that the cotton crop failed two years in a row due to insects and disease. We didn't even plant cotton this year. We planted yellow beans instead, but cotton brings in more than twice as much money.[3] Selling cotton has been our main source of cash. We make nothing from our wheat. After putting aside part of the wheat harvest for seed and for taxes, there is only enough left to eat. Only wheat is taxed; cotton is not, so we have relied on cotton to pay our expenses.

Tax policy has changed since your last visit, and the amount of tax we have to pay has increased. The government asks too much and gives too little. From 1991 to 1993, every household had to pay 190 jin of wheat per person regardless of how much they grew.[4] That was about one-third of the total wheat harvest and about 10 percent of our total income. We also pay a special products tax on our date trees and various village taxes for things like education, militia training, road repair, irrigation, family planning, and aid to dependents in soldiers' families. Everyone pays the same tax, so some families are a lot better off than others.

There was so much complaint about the wheat tax that in 1994 it was reduced to 107 jin per person, and the special products tax was tripled. That was done to make the tax burden more equitable between villages that produce more or less wheat and dates. What it amounted to was that in 1994 our total tax per person was 55 yuan, or about 8 percent of our per capita income. That may not seem to be a very high percentage to you, but 55 yuan is a lot of money for farmers when their total income is only 700 yuan, which is hardly enough to live on before taxes. We consider the tax high. Furthermore, we think our grain is worth more than the government says it is. The government grain monopoly sets the price. We are not allowed to trade grain on the open market. We can sell it to individuals, but not to nongovernment grain traders.

Taxes, except those that stay in the village, are collected by township officials. They keep some of it and send the rest to higher levels of government. I do not know what percentage each level gets. I do not know if there is corruption in the process of tax collection.[5] But people are angry at the government because it gives nothing back for our tax payments. The government today doesn't care about the farmer. There are no policies to benefit agriculture.[6] Fertilizer and electricity prices rise all the time. About a month ago, the price for a ton of fertilizer rose from 1,200 to 1,700 yuan. Electricity now costs 485 yuan per kilowatt hour, much higher than it was a few years ago. I don't know whether the government controls the prices of fertilizer and electricity anymore, but people blame the government for increases.

Wang Fucheng:
I'll give you an example of how the government favors the cities over the villages. My retirement pension from the government for having been village Party secretary for thirty years is only 200 yuan per year. That is half the amount that my son Dejun gets for being Party secretary now. Retirement pay for village cadres is half the amount they would have received in their former positions. Until last year, I also received an extra 200 yuan for my health. If I had gone to work for the Party in the city years ago, I would be getting thirteen months' salary and rice. I have a cousin who lived in this village and is illiterate, like me. Years ago, I helped him get a job in the city. He is now retired and gets 500 yuan per month. He also gets a rice allowance and health benefits from his former work unit.[7] Some other people from this village who went to the city as unskilled workers now get 300 yuan per month retirement pay. A young nephew who recently graduated from high school now works for the Capital Steel Company in Beijing. He makes 600 yuan a month. Compare that to our 700 yuan per year.

In the past, village people were not allowed to move to the city to find work. You had to have a residence certificate, and that was almost impossible to get. Some people from this village got them because they were helped by my uncle Wang Congwu. Today it is still hard to get an urban residence certificate, but the government does not have as much control as it used to have. Most young men who leave the village to find work today become "public project workers" (*min gong*). They build roads, rail lines, public buildings, and so on. The work is very hard, and the living conditions are poor. Most live in tents or makeshift huts near the construction site. They eat mostly noodles and are paid only 10 yuan a day, but that is about 300 yuan a month, much more than they can make in the village.

In 1951 I had a chance to work on the railroad near Beijing. In fact, I went there for one month. Conditions were very difficult. We lived in wild, open fields. The food was better than in the village—we ate wheat rather than corn—but the living conditions were worse. After a month, I returned home. The main reason I returned is that my mind was on the village. I was determined to make the village prosperous. The other reason is that my uncle Wang Congwu told me that because I was illiterate I had no future working for the railroad. He wanted me to return home and take care of family and village affairs. I am glad that I returned. This village became better off than other villages around here.

Wang Dejun:

We may not make as much money as city workers, but we have a better life. We work for ourselves. In the days of collective agriculture, when the commune told us what to do, we worked more days, but we did not work as hard. Now we work very hard during the two busy months in the spring and fall when we harvest crops and plant new seeds, but the rest of the time we can relax. There are six months in the winter when we don't work at all. We play cards and mahjong. Do we get bored? Why should we get bored with playing?

Still, there is great uncertainty in farming. Currently our standard of living is declining. We are very worried about the future. The county government wants us to develop new enterprises in the village. A few weeks ago I traveled to Qingdao and Yantai [in Shandong Province] and other areas looking for good projects where they have had success in creating new enterprises. The trip was not useful. The projects required materials that we don't have or required a lot of capital. It is almost impossible to borrow capital from banks now.[8] The county and township government keep telling us to use our own funds, but we do not have any funds. Very few people in this village have savings. Most do not make enough to save. They spend it on fertilizer, insecticides, education, and medicine. If they have any left over, they spend it on clothes and other personal items. There is not much point in putting savings in banks because banks pay only 1.5 percent interest per year. When families do save, it is for weddings and funerals. A wedding costs the groom's family about 6,000 yuan, a full year's income for most households. In this area, the groom's family pays all the expenses for the wedding. They must buy new furniture and other gifts and pay the brides's family. Funerals can be very expensive, too. We simply do not have the money to invest in enterprises, but they keep insisting.

I'll show you a proclamation that I received yesterday from a government office in Anyang City.[9] It says that this village is to invest 50,000 yuan this year in an enterprise that will produce 400,000 yuan worth of products each year. To enforce the order, the Party secretary is supposed to make a deposit of 200 yuan of his own money. He will forfeit the deposit if there is not an enterprise plan by August, if work on the project has not begun by October, and if production is not underway by December. Furthermore, the Party secretary will be demoted to vice secretary, and the police will investigate his property if these deadlines are not met. This is just another trick by the government to get people involved. It is just a show. No one takes it seriously. I won't give a deposit of 200 yuan, and they won't do anything about it. The purpose is just to try to show officials at a higher level that they are serious.

I don't know what we will do eventually. We may start a chicken farm, or bottle our underground water for sale. Whatever I do, I will do it very carefully. There are many cheaters around these days who will take your money and run away. Village people have been cheated too much in the past. If you invest the farmers' money and lose it, they will get very angry. It is not easy to be a leader in these situations. You live in the same village all your life. You don't want to make enemies because resentments remain.

Wang Fucheng:
The risk involved in starting an enterprise can be seen in what happened to the brick kiln in this village. When you were last here, the managers of the brick kiln were making a lot of money. In 1992, management of the kiln came up for bid again. Four households won the bid for 24,000 yuan for two years. They lost money and had to ask the village for an extra year to make up the loss. The leaders granted their request. This year the kiln management was up for bid again. Only two households bid, and their bid was only 12,000 yuan. The kiln lost money because of poor management and also because the price of coal, electricity, and labor all went up. It is also because the soil for making bricks is not as good here as it is in some other places. We did not use the local bricks when we built our house. But the main problem was management. It was not a lack of demand for bricks. Even though most families in this area have already built new houses, they

now want to enlarge them. And newly married couples want to build their own houses. The population is still growing, and we are still losing farm land to new buildings.

Wang Dejun:

Population control is still the main concern of the Party in this area. The number one priority for farmers is to have a boy. Farmers depend on boys for their labor and for support in their old age. Girls marry and move out of the village, leaving the family powerless. So if a family's only child is a girl, they still want a boy very much. Some pregnant women flee the village so that they will not be forced to have an abortion. To prevent that, the government policy in the past two years has been to seize everyone in her family and try to make them bring her back for an abortion. If that fails, the township government will levy a heavy fine or tear down the family's house. The fine used to be 4,000 yuan. It is now 6,800 yuan. Those who cannot pay the fine are arrested and forced to borrow from relatives and friends or to sign an agreement to pay in installments. If they do not pay, they are arrested again and put in jail.

In this village no houses have been destroyed, but I know of five or six houses that have been destroyed in other villages in this township. Our son, Yanwei, has worked on family planning for the township for the past two years. I know that he helped dismantle a house in Liu Village. This happens only with the third or fourth child. With the second child, the family is just fined. Also, dismantling happens only when the family has fled and the house is empty. If people are still there, they will try other methods first.[10]

Wang Fucheng:

In the old days the village government was more powerful and could handle these problems itself. The Party organization in the village is even weaker now than it was when you were here before. There are still about forty Party members, but they don't meet at all anymore. The three members in the Party committee met only twice last year, at the [lunar] New Year and on August 1.[11]

Wang Dejun:

On August 1 we sit in the field, eat watermelon, and discuss things. Last year we discussed birth control and how much money the village should collect for things like the school. When the Party sends announcements to the village, I read them over the village loudspeaker rather than call a meeting. If there are important matters to discuss, representatives from households that share an irrigation well in a field will come together to discuss them.

Wang Fucheng:

With the decline of the authority of the Party and government, crime has been a continually increasing problem. I have heard that in Wei County, just north of here in Hebei Province, the military came in and took over the county government because there were so many bandit gangs.[12]

Wang Dejun:

That problem is not confined to Wei County. In Neihuang County there are bandit gangs too—in Tianshi, Songcun, and Chuwang townships there are bandit gangs. Those townships all border Hebei Province. In the border area along Hebei, Shandong, and Henan provinces, there are a lot of bandits because they can move between provinces easily and escape local police forces. These gangs are very dangerous. They have weapons. They stop travelers in trucks, buses, and taxis and rob them. Buses particularly are stopped, and everyone on them is robbed. Those who resist are often killed. It is called "cutting the road" (*duan dao* or *jie lu*). Your taxi driver from Anyang yesterday said that Neihuang County is a very dangerous place. He said he wouldn't stop to pick up anyone on the way home because it is too risky. He said he would roll up the windows and lock the doors and drive back to Anyang as fast as possible.

On the whole, this area has less crime than surrounding areas because officials in Liucun Township are tough. They punish severely and do not allow a trend to develop. Some property, such as TV sets, is stolen. I keep equipment like loudspeakers and things from the family temple here in our house, or they would be stolen. But, the thieves are individuals, not gang members. Usually the thieves are from outside the village, but they have people in the village helping them.

We did have one incident with a gang recently. One night last winter a gang from Dongzhuang Township came to Houhua and stole thirty or forty goats from thirty or forty households. They came in a truck, grabbed the goats, and ran. We found out that the bandits were from Dongzhuang and called the county police. The bandits were arrested, but people here were very angry when the police asked them to pay to get the goats back. Some paid, but some didn't and just gave up their goats rather than go to additional trouble and expense. We do not know what happened to the bandits. It is not legal for the police to charge for their services, and it is not common here, but corruption is increasing everywhere.

The farmers in Chairman Mao's time had a greater sense of safety and security than they have now. Even though we did not have enough to eat in Mao's time, we still thought Mao was great. Now we have enough to eat, but everyone curses Deng Xiaoping because there is no security and too much corruption. We have little hope for the future of the village because of corruption.

Wang Fucheng:

Security is very important for farmers. Prices change so much today that there is no certainty. In Chairman Mao's time, there was more certainty. In those days, the government stressed agriculture and made a real attempt to help agriculture. There were no fake fertilizers and fake insecticides. So much of it is fake today. Today the government talks a lot about agriculture, but it does nothing to help the farmer. But as much as the farmers complain, they do not want to go back to the old system. They have more money now and more freedom. They do not like the uncertainty, but they do not want to go back. There is hope for the village in the future if the government gives us more help—more loans, more fertilizer. That is what we need.

Wang Dejun:

Hope for the village is conditional. If the central government reduces the burden on farmers and helps us start new enterprises, there is hope. Without that there is not much hope. In the near future I see little significant change. There is no trend toward mechanization of agriculture. There is no capital to start new industries. The only way farmers can improve their lives is to sell their labor cheap to people in cities. There is not much hope in that.

We think a lot about the future of our children. Yanwei is twenty now [nineteen by Western reckoning]. He will not be a farmer. For the past two years he has worked for the township government on family planning. He is officially registered as a government worker now, a state employee, not a farmer. He gets a salary from the state and does not get a share of land in the village. He didn't finish junior high school because he didn't like it. He hopes to get a correspondence degree from the Anyang Party School. If he gets it, he might be elevated to official (*ganbu*) status. Currently he works seven days a week and sometimes at night, mostly filling in forms for the county government. He is paid 100 yuan a month, but he spends more than that and asks his mother for money. Even though he is not paid much, it is more than he could make from farming now that the cotton crop has failed.

Yanwei is engaged to be married. He will be married at the end of this year. You are invited to the wedding. He is younger than the official age for marriage (which is twenty-two), so we will have to pay a fine of 1,000 yuan to the township. Most people in the village marry early and have to pay the fine. We get no special treatment.

Yanwei's fiancée is from Dongzhuang Village, not far from here. He was introduced to her by a go-between, a woman who used to live in Houhua before she married a man from Dongzhuang. The fiancée is in a three-year program in the Neihuang medical school. She will graduate next year.

Yanwei:

I see this girl about once a month. I don't like her much. There is a girl from this village who I like.

Li Suzhen, Yanwei's mother:

The girl from this village is trying to win Yanwei over. We do not like her very much because of the way she speaks and acts. She flirts a lot and dresses too flashy.

Yanwei:

I don't want to get married soon. My parents can't make that decision for me. They can make decisions about other things, but not that.

Li Suzhen:

Our daughters are not engaged yet, though it is customary in the village for girls to be engaged by age fifteen or sixteen. Yanxia is now in a teacher training school. She plans to teach elementary school. Why don't you take her to America with you? Yongxia is in junior secondary school. She has no career plans yet. If she does well, she may go to high school in the county. Both girls like school, but they do not like to work in the fields. When they go to the fields, they just read books and don't do any work.

I do most of the farm work now. My husband is often busy with Party secretary work, Yanwei works for the township, the girls are useless in the fields, and my in-laws have retired. We have lent out six of the family's 13 mu of agricultural fields to a relative in exchange for him paying all our taxes. We have also joined a cooperative group of four families who help each other at harvest time. We share two oxen and tools in addition to labor. So you see, most of the family is already out of farming. The future is uncertain, but our children's lives will be very different from ours.

Wang Fucheng:

And what of your future? Will you be coming back to Houhua? We hope that you and your family will return and that everyone will stay longer next time. I know that conditions in the village are poor and that we cannot treat you adequately, but we have been friends for over seven years. We call each other brother. We are like one family.

Postscript

Wang Fucheng died in April 1995. His son, Wang Dejun, wrote to inform me that his father had succumbed to the effects of a massive stroke, and that his mother, Wang Xianghua, had also suffered a stroke a week later, leaving her seriously disabled. This sad news made me reflect on Wang Fucheng's parting words to me: In important ways we were like one family. I had developed a genuine affection for Wang Fucheng and Wang Xianghua. I had learned much from them, not just about rural China but also about friendship, trust, and human decency.

Notes

Preface

1. "War of Resistance" is the term used in China to refer to what most of the rest of the world calls World War II. In China the war lasted eight years, following the Japanese attack in north China on July 7, 1937.

2. Since then, there has been an excellent study by Odoric Y.K. Wou, *Mobilizing the Masses: Building Revolution in Henan* (Stanford: Stanford University Press, 1994).

3. The colleague is Ralph Thaxton, a professor of political science at Brandeis University. I am much indebted to him for his ingenuity and persistence in negotiating admission to the area.

4. See, for instance, numerous accounts recorded by former *New York Times* correspondents Nicholas Kristof and Sheryl WuDunn in their book *China Wakes* (New York: Time Books, Random House, 1994).

5. In 1994, I was assisted by Han Dongping, also an instructor at Zhengzhou University. Both Han and Li later came to the United States. They both earned master's degrees in history at the University of Vermont and then went on to study for Ph.D. degrees at Brandeis University and the University of Minnesota, respectively.

6. See, for instance, Edward Friedman, Paul Pickowicz, and Mark Selden, *Chinese Village, Socialist State* (New Haven: Yale University Press. 1991).

Introduction

1. Han is the largest of the more than fifty ethnic groups in China today. It constitutes approximately 94 percent of the total population.

2. Cao Kun, Wu Peifu, Feng Yuxiang, and Zhang Zuolin.

Chapter One

1. Yan Xishan controlled all of Shanxi Province at the time. Shanxi abuts the northwest boundary of Henan Province.

2. Jiang's strategy was to "trade space for time"; thus he did abandon some areas without a fight, but he fought in others in the early years of the war. Ding Shuben did, in fact, resist the Japanese briefly before withdrawing from the Neihuang area.

Chapter Two

1. Sun Buyue, the leader of a religious sect, had collaborated with the Japanese during the war (see Chapter 1). Under Japanese auspices, he controlled Hua and Xun Counties to the south of Neihuang County.

2. Even at that low figure, Houhua produced twice the average for Neihuang County. See introductory chapter.

3. The United Defense Brigade was made up of combined village militia units. In creating these units, the Communists were following a practice established in the 1920s. See introductory chapter.

Chapter Three

1. "Face" here means pride and respect.

Chapter Four

1. Distributing the harvest on the basis of need rather than on the basis of work was encouraged early in the "Leap" as a way to accelerate progress from socialism to communism; that is, to put into practice Marx's definition of a communist state as one that observes the formula "from each according to ability, to each according to need." As Wang Fucheng indicated, the work-point system soon replaced the idealistic free supply system.

Chapter Five

1. For instance, see accounts of this campaign in two other village studies: Anita Chan, et al., *Chen Village* (Berkeley: University of California Press, 1984); and Shumin Huang, *The Spiral Road* (Boulder, CO: Westview Press, 1989).

2. Lei Feng was said to have been a soldier in the People's Liberation Army. He was noted for his selfless, untiring service to the people, a character trait that he was said to have acquired and sustained by regularly reading the works of Chairman Mao. He was used recurrently (as late as 1990) by the Communist Party as an emulation model for the youth of the whole country.

3. The first four cleanups, or Small Four Cleanups, were to clean up, or straighten out, wages, accounts, store houses, and property.

4. The Big Four Cleanups were more comprehensive and more vague. They focused on politics, economics, ideology, and organization. As in the Five Winds campaign, the struggle in the villages reflected a more crucial struggle at the top between Mao and his detractors.

Chapter Six

1. A seal, usually carved in stone, has always had enormous significance in China. No proclamation, even an imperial proclamation, was considered legitimate unless stamped with an official seal. Seals were carefully guarded, for they represented the authority of office.

2. Revolutionary Committees were organizations set up to reestablish order after Party and government organs had been destroyed in the early phase of the Cultural Revolution. The formula for their composition was "3 in 1." That is, they were sup-

posed to incorporate diverse elements in the community in which they were being formed. Those elements would differ from place to place. Typically in a village they would include representatives of former cadres, new radical leaders, and "poor and lower-middle peasants" [peasants who had been relatively impoverished before land reform]. They would also include young, middle-aged, and old representatives. Such committees in urban areas were established in factories, universities, and former government offices. There they were usually dominated by units of the People's Liberation Army, or by paramilitary organizations called Mao Zedong Thought Worker Propaganda Teams.

3. "Lower-middle" peasants were those who before land reform were self-sufficient peasants, but only barely. They were on the margin of slipping into poor-peasant status, meaning that they would have to farm as tenants on the land of rich peasants or landlords to support their families (see the introduction to Chapter 3 for a fuller explanation of social categories in rural areas). The Communist Party considered poor and lower-middle peasants to be their most reliable allies.

4. The Three Venerable Articles are short pieces included in the canon of Mao's *Selected Works*. They were said to represent the essence of his ideology. They are "Serve the People," "In Memory of Norman Bethune," and "The Foolish Old Man Who Removed the Mountain." They extol selflessness, hard work, internationalism, and faith in the ability of the masses to accomplish any task, no matter how difficult.

5. The official account of Lin Biao's death is that his plane crashed in Inner Mongolia, having run out of gas before reaching its intended destination, the USSR. Many people are skeptical of this official account.

6. Zhengzhou is the capitol of Henan Province. Wang Fucheng's remark reveals how ignorant he is of politics at the national level.

7. Dazhai Brigade, in Shaanxi Province, was an emulation model for self-reliance. Once an impoverished village, it became self-sufficient and even somewhat prosperous, ostensibly through the creative efforts and hard work of the local citizens under the leadership of Party secretary Chen Yonggui. Following the end of the Cultural Revolution, it was revealed that Dazhai was a fake, that in fact this "model of self-reliance" had benefitted from large amounts of government aid designed to make the model appear to be all the more glorious. The choice of emulation models in China is significant. It demonstrates authority. Dazhai, like other emulation models, was a vehicle in a power struggle at the highest levels of the Party and government. It symbolized Mao's advocacy of local economic self-reliance in opposition to those who favored an economy more integrated and open nationally and internationally.

8. The distribution system at Dazhai brigade was supposedly closer to the communist ideal than the system that had been used in most of the country after collectivization. At Dazhai, families were supplied with their basic needs, and the remaining surplus was distributed after public discussion and collective decision. By contrast, distribution in Houhua Village and in most other villages was based on a ten-point work assessment system. See Wang Fucheng's remarks on this in Chapter 3.

9. The three categories into which villages are divided are (1) those that produce a surplus, (2) those that are self-sufficient after paying taxes, and (3) those that can-

not afford to pay taxes or that need government help. Houhua Village was in category 3 in the early years of the People's Republic and is currently in category 2.

10. In numerous campaigns during the course of their tenure of power in China the leadership of the Communist Party sent cadres to lower levels for varied amounts of time to observe conditions, use their talents on behalf of the local populace, and improve their ideological disposition by learning from workers and peasants.

11. Zhou Enlai's remains were cremated and scattered over China from the air. Even though the Communist Party had always advocated cremation, in the interest of economy and space, such a procedure is difficult for peasants to accept because of the continuing traditional Chinese belief that a body should be buried whole after death. See Chapter 10 for a fuller discussion of village death rites and beliefs.

12. It was Mao's wish to be interred at Eight Treasures Mountain, the official burial place for revolutionary heroes and martyrs, but he instead was embalmed and put on display in a specially built mausoleum in Tiananmen Square.

Chapter Seven

1. The brick factory, in fact, did not do well in the early 1990s. By 1993 the new owners were losing money. See Chapter 11.

2. "Barefoot doctors" were residents of a village who normally engaged in farm work and acted as medical workers when the need arose. Usually, they had very little, if any, formal medical training.

3. The terminology "five guarantees" is left over from the Great Leap Forward period, when the government, in its effort to hasten the advent of a truly communist era, guaranteed each household food, clothing, shelter, education, and a decent burial.

4. By 1994 the government store had closed for lack of sufficient business.

Chapter Eight

1. Wang Fucheng's use of the term "class" indicates what had happened to the term in China under the leadership of Mao Zedong. It no longer referred to social relations determined by the "mode of production" as in Marx, but had come to refer to social relations determined by more subjective concepts such as "advanced" or "backward"; those concepts were determined by whether one agreed or disagreed with the current policies of the current leadership.

2. See Chapter 5 for previous discussion of Lei Feng.

Chapter Ten

1. There have been a number of books published in the 1990s that have been highly critical of Mao. See particularly Li Zhisui, *The Private Life of Chairman Mao* (New York: Random House, 1994).

2. In the four years that had elapsed since my last visit to China, Chinese currency had been devalued considerably vis-à-vis the U.S. dollar. The summer 1994 rate was US$1 = RMB 8.7.

3. Wang Dejun told me that they harvest about 300–400 jin of beans per mu and sell them for 0.90–1.00 yuan per jin. Cotton plants produce about 160 jin of raw cotton per mu and sell at 5.00 yuan per jin. Thus, taking an average of harvest and price, 1 mu of beans would bring an income of 332.50 yuan, and the same area planted with cotton would bring 800 yuan, or nearly 60 percent more.

4. Compare this with the tax policy in 1990 described in Chapter 9.

5. There have been numerous reports from other parts of China that local governments often raise taxes arbitrarily and illegally and keep the money to invest in local projects owned, or managed, by local officials. In 1994, the central government officially rebuked those engaging in such practices, indicating the pervasiveness of the problem.

6. This statement is an exaggeration. There are a number of agricultural measures in effect, but it is apparent that Wang Dejun finds them inadequate.

7. Those health benefits often exist only on paper. It is up to each unit to determine what health benefits it is able, or willing, to pay. Often it is very difficult for even those people ostensibly covered by the government health system to get care without a "back door" relationship with someone in authority, or without giving a "gift" to induce a favor.

8. The national government had forbidden bank loans for most village and township enterprises because many had not been successful and were adding to serious inflation problems. Inflation in the summer of 1994 was running over 25 percent.

9. Houhua Village is under the jurisdiction of Anyang municipality. The municipality is a jurisdictional level subordinate to the province. It incorporates all counties, townships, and villages within a given area.

10. Wang Dejun is ambiguous in this remark. I had heard accounts from other places in northern Henan describing the destruction of houses when the family was still in residence. Policies are implemented differently in different places and depend on the decision of the local leadership.

11. August 1 (*ba yi*) is a holiday celebrating the founding of the Red Army on that date in 1927.

12. In pre-Communist times, Wei County was notorious for its bandit gangs.

About the Book and Author

This engaging book sketches an intimate portrait of the life of Wang Fucheng, an illiterate peasant who served for thirty years as Communist Party secretary of an impoverished village on the north China plain. Based on conversations over a seven-year period (1987–1994) between Wang Fucheng and Peter Seybolt, the book unfolds as a continuous first-person narrative, framed by the author's overview and chapter introductions.

Born in 1923, Wang Fucheng rose under the Communists from extreme poverty to a position of power and prestige in his village. His account provides a fascinating illustration of the process of social mobility during the Maoist era, the interaction between central and local leaders, and the way central policies were adapted at the village level. The book's compelling and evocative picture of life in rural China will appeal to scholars, students, and general readers alike.

Peter J. Seybolt is professor of history and director of the Asian Studies Program at the University of Vermont.